Beautiful
SWITZERLAND
Bernese Oberland

BEAUTIFUL
SWITZERLAND
BERNESE OBERLAND

Photos: Martin Thomas
Text: Sergius Golowin
Gertrude Reinisch

Contents

Page 2: Folk vocalists in the Bernese Oberland.

Left: View from the platform of the Kabinenberg railway station onto the Männlichen. On the left, the Breithorn (3782 m).

Page 6/7: View from Niesen to the lake of Thun.

Alpine Walk through the Centuries

An Emblem which the Whole World Knows

The whole world knows about the Bernese Oberland, even those countless people, who never heard the name, either in history or geography: If one speaks of Switzerland, or perhaps merely of the mountain range, the Alps, which divide Europe into North and South, then almost all call the same tremendous picture to mind: the three snow-capped, rocky giants, which stand together in a unified whole.

The names of the mountains, irrevocably linked as they are, are as famous as this great natural picture: The *Eiger*, which even from the distance appears threateningly dangerous, notoriously gruelling for mountain climbers, the *Mönch*, which, in contrast, appears appealingly wide, and finally the gleaming *Jungfrau*, which has almost become a trademark for our country. For centuries people have been coming to see these three great mountains and they have become a symbol for the beauty of creation in the reveries of poets and in countless paintings.

Whether it was on horseback, in their carriages, or later by rail, scarcely had the travellers arrived in the capital Bern, situated on the mountain river Aare, when they hastened off to the favourable vantage points to view the Bernese Alps. Occasionally, they were disappointed by gloomy weather, by low clouds which concealed the Oberland. Yet, astonishingly often they found what they had awaited. In this picturesque town, with its almost complete medieval setting, shielded from the harsher traits of the climate by its leafy canopy, the fairy tale picture rises up: before a blue sky, flooded with the gold of the gleaming sun, the three great mountains, known to everyone.

If the weather is good and, like the alpine pilgrims and wayfarers of times gone by, one is not in too much of a hurry, one can approach this wonder of creation slowly. From the town of Bern our path leads along the river Aare, which flows down from the Alps, towards the small town of Thun, the gateway, so to speak, to the Oberland proper. If one is lucky enough to have a fine, sunny day for the journey, one can see the picture of the three alpine giants stretch out into an ever mightier semi-circle, growing into the heights, as if the whole of the mountain countryside were ready to receive us.

Old legends from the Oberland tell how an immortal wayfarer roams across the lofty mountain passes of Grimsel or Brünig every hundred or even thousand years – each time he discovers astonishing changes in the landscape. At one point he passes a sun-lit slope, full of ripening vines, which promise to bring forth exquisite wine. Then he sees sumptuous meadows with cows, which thanks to the wonderful grass, produce the very best milk. On the same spot a hundred years later he finds only cold, barren cliffs without any sign of life …

And so we see that long before research into the earth's evolution brought results, the mountain shepherds were thinking about the transformation of their world! And it is almost impossible to rid oneself of such ideas in the Alps: The richness of the seasons, the glorious summer, the spring with the first blossoms, the winter which compresses all existence with its dense white cover – all these are normally separated by months. In the Oberland mountains, which are symbolised by the Eiger, Mönch and Jungfrau, all these seasons can be encountered in some places in an ascent of only a few hours duration.

As if by magic the cable railway hovers in the immediate vicinity of the Ice-Age glacier and then soon over regions full of green; the god-fearing inhabitants once said of these regions that the Creator himself had «taken earth from his Paradise» to form them.

Oberland Legends about Cow Grazing and Wholesome Milk

Most people who travel through the Bernese Oberland still expect today to be greeted immediately by the «classic» view, known to them from old pictures or the tales of their grandparents. The picture of the resting or grazing cows, which characterizes the landscape, is as

The Lauterbrunnen valley, from the Wengen forest looking towards the Breithorn (3782 m).

Looking from the landing stage at Brienz towards the north west and the Hasli valley.

popular as the view of the summits of the eternally snow-capped Eiger, Mönch and Jungfrau.

In olden times, the whole of Switzerland was a land of shepherds and if the inhabitants of the various valleys knew how to win and preserve a certain independence, this was often enough ascribed to the «strength» which their cattle farming imbued them with. It is a later Bernese chronicler, Hans Rudolf Grimm (1665–1749), who connects the once prover-bial «power» of his compatriots fully with their cow farming. He says: «As far as the Swiss way of life is concerned, this has changed substantially amongst the aristocracy and the burghers (the better families of the town are meant here), for the aristocracy and burghers no longer pay so much attention to cheese and dairy products as they once did. [...] And so because of this change [...] there are no longer such tall and strong people, as there were in olden times and (the people) do not live as long.»

Such stories about cows, milk and cheese were again and again regarded as the real secret of Switzer-land, and attempts were continually made in the European countries to take over this natural national richness and spread it throughout Europe. As early as the eighteenth century a beautiful tale was put about and taken seriously: a famous king liked the mountain cheese from the Alps, and so the tale goes, he decided to give it a new home in his kingdom.

Was he the King of France or of Prussia? Perhaps it was the Tsar of faraway Russia? It can have been anyone of these, because it is known that at that time all of these rulers admired Switzerland and the world of the mountains, at least from the time on when the Bernese poet and doctor, Albrecht von Haller, in his book «Alpen» and then also Jean-Jacques Rousseau, the nature-lover from Geneva, sang their praises like of a lost paradise ...

But let us continue with the beautiful and appar-ently true story in the version that I found in the old Bernese book about the shepherds. The good king, who so loved the tasty cheese, called some of the most experienced and diligent cowherds from their home-land. They came, were pleased with their good wage and began their usual work – however, what they produced with their milk, did not please the disap-pointed ruler particularly.

«You can't have Swiss cheese without the right cows!» the worthy experts from the highlands now explained to the king. With a sigh, the latter agreed with his advisers and, not without much ado and expense, sent for the animals from their home – probably from the Simmen valley, Saan valley and from another valley, well known for its good cattle.

Now the cowherds were there, the best cheese makers from the Oberland and their cattle with their large udders; however, the dairy products which were prepared, still did not meet with royal expectations. The experts from the pastoral land considered the possible sources for this failure, pondered a while and finally explained: «Your Majesty, we have come to the conclusion, that we can now produce our cheese without further ado in this kingdom, if our mountains are brought in …»

It is likely that the ruler lacked the necessary wherewithal for the continuation of his experiment. However, since then one thing is certain and can no doubt be seen as a summary of this whole book: It is impossible to single out one part from the wealth of details which belong to the Bernese Oberland in order to explain its continuing impact. Somehow everything belongs together: the view of the mountains and the

In Iseltwald, the south eastern road along the bank of the lake of Brienz comes to an end.

elements which have been shaping the landscape for thousands of years, the cows, grazing freely in a circle around the alpine huts, the people with their rich history.

On the Tracks of the Migration of Peoples

As early as the end of the Middle Ages an attempt was made to bring a little order into the legends surrounding the origins of the Oberland people. There seem to have been thousands of these legends. In these legends the inhabitants of the neighbouring valley could appear as people of a completely different race and the people from very far away regions as blood relations.

I possess a copy of the poet Fritz Ringgenberg von Meiringen's beautiful book «Sie sägen, das vor alten Zyten …» («They say that long ago …»). In his dedication he kindly calls me «the spiritual father» of his book – and this is «only» based on a pleasant experience that we both had in Haslital in 1963: Over a glass of wine a mountain dweller whom he knew told us the story of «King Gisbertus of Sweden and Count Christoffel of Friesland», who migrated here from the North with the ancestors of the alpine farmers.

I was so taken with the vividness of the tale of the two heroes, that I thought this tale had to be written down as accurately as possible! «This is superfluous,» said the mountain dweller, «everyone who is involved knows the story only too well – and the others don't believe it anyway.» Fritz Ringgenberg then published the legend in the dialect of the Haslital, but sometimes I think that our source was right about a lot of things.

Melchior Sooder, who collects legends, also told me about the legend which states that the Fresians are the forefathers of the population of Habkern. Moreover, he presumes that the monastery at Interlaken and the barons living around the lakes of Thun and Brienz, through their connections, actually attracted settlers «from all possible wind directions». The old name «Wandelsee», as the lake of Thun was once called, was earlier popularly attributed to the Germanic Vandals or the Slavic Wends – both peoples are often confused in the tales of old chroniclers.

Eulogius Kyberger and Rebmann von Thun, who give a good picture of the mountain legends of the 15th and 16th century in their writings, assume that the tower of the castle at Spiez was built by Attila, the King of the Huns. According to an appealing legend, which probably stems from these two chroniclers, this «ruler above all rulers» governed his empire from the lake of Thun, with the aid of fire signals on the mountains.

It is possible that in these stories about the Huns in the Bernese Oberland, there is some confusion with Hungary, which at that time was still heathen and which advanced as far as the Alps in the 10th century. According to more or less reliable sources, they are said to have fought against the Islamic Saracens, who attempted to open up the heart of Europe from the Mediterranean Sea – as is well known, they did not succeed.

The Saracens, who came from Spain and the Mediterranean, are said to have left their traces behind in the Alps: Occasionally the beautiful, dark girls, who can be seen in many of the mountain valleys and who are the pride of the Oberland, are declared to be the great-grandchildren of these daring «Moors». (At one point I heard another interpretation for their appearance: Many women from the Orient came with the mercenary army of Duke Karl the Brave as he advanced on Bern in 1476; thanks to the knight from Spiez, Adrian von Bubenberg, he was then defeated. These women fell to the Confederates as «booty», became their wives and the great-grandmothers of many of the dark indigenous people.

However, the confusing legends about the origins of the Oberland had significant consequences especially in the 18th and 19th century. German, Hungarian, Polish and Russian refugees in Switzerland became interested in the legends and saw a mysterious relation to their lost homelands in the hospitable inhabitants of the individual valley communities. Even today the traditional tales of the Saracens in the Alps, which are understandably enough being newly discovered by Arab writers for their people, are said to have very much pleased at least some of the oil sheikhs visiting the area.

Independent of the value of the individual stories about Huns, Irish, Romans, Greeks, Goths, Swedes, Slavs as the ancestors of certain families, this group of legends is the expression of a sentiment that the guest in the Alps can have: Many a one of them finds landscapes that do not appear alien to him; on the contrary, he can not ward off the impression that «somehow he has returned home».

Early Christian Legends

The inhabitants of the Oberland regard the first century of the Christian calendar as one of the great golden ages of their country of lakes and mountains. St. Beatus, who according to legend came from Celtic England or even Sweden, is said to have belonged to one of the first heralders of the new faith. It is said that while still a young man searching for the truth, he had been directed in his dreams to wander towards and that the Apostel Peter baptised him personally.

He is said to have entered the Oberland across the Brünig pass with his pious companion, Justus. They even brought their teachings to the villages on the Lake of Brienz, and some tales depict the landscape at this time almost as a refuge for the best and most devout people of the time: The godlessness in the capital, Rome, is said to have driven many of the families, who suffered under the tyranny and the arbitrariness of unjust officials, to the valleys of the Alps. Here they were content; Beatus and Justus gave them comfort and promised them a better future.

The two then travelled on to the Northern bank of the lake of Thun, crossing the Bödeli, where Interlaken stands today. Here St. Beatus drove an horrific dragon out of the famous caves, which still bear his name. One of the early scholars saw a symbol for pre-Christian religion in the «flying snake» which recoiled before the

The Giessbach falls. The water masses cascade about four hundred metres into the lake of Brienz.

herald of Christianity: In the 19th century a clergyman in Beatenberg, G. Dummermuth, collected legends connected with this and was even convinced that they possessed a core of truth. The cave, «unique as it was», was formed by nature in such a way that it was completely suitable for the worship of the divine hero, Mithras, who in the last centuries of the Celtic-Roman era had continually grown in significance and tradition.

According to the enduring legend of the Bernese Oberland these first early Christians of the Alps knew how to adapt the best side of pre-Christian piousness to the new era. Beatus and Justus are said to have befriended the earth spirits, «the blessed little people», living in the rocks. The pastor Dummermuth confirmed this continuing tradition in 1889. «As once the prophet Elia was eaten by ravens, they (the little mountain people) took care of our apostle's physical well-being». And so it was that, in alliance with his «blessed little people», he enabled the survival of the first Christians, refugees from the Roman cities, who were partly accustomed to luxury. When these refugees fell asleep at night, the little «mountain people» are said to have come into their huts at night and «brought them help». This enabled them to find food in the alpine countryside the next day without great trouble.

It was also the «blessed little people» who disclosed all the secrets of the indigenous herbs to St. Beatus; these were brought to him, it is said, by his wonderful «gnomes» even from the highest summit, or from the immediacy of the perennial ice. It was thus that the fine man managed to take care of both the mental and physical health of the Christian community, which grew in his domain.

Beatus is said to have worked mainly in the region of Sundlauenen, but, thanks to his wonderful coat, was also easily able to cross the lake of Thun, to preach in the ancient church of Einigen. According to tradition, St. Justus, his companion, settled in the nearby Justi valley. A legend also states that the apostles knew every secret path thanks to the mountain gnomes, and so Justus carried on his teachings between Sigriswil and Alp Seefeld ob Habkern – which are said to have been more populated in the days of early Christianity than now.

In the 16th century the Reformation prohibited this place of pilgrimage, probably one of the most popular in the whole of the Alps – naturally not without the sorrow and opposition of the indigenous population. The belief that the Bernese Oberland was a focuspoint for early Christianity, as expressed in this legend, is today taken more seriously than in the century of a superficially understood «Enlightenment».

Bertha's «Golden Age»

In the 15th century the pastor Eulogius Kyburger completed a chronicle, which dealt with the noble clan of the Stretlinger (Strättliger). Although they were supposed to have had a strong influence on the historical picture of the Oberland, they had been regarded as nothing less than a collection of phantasies, a wreath of legends woven around Beatus and Justus. Yet it seems almost unthinkable to me that a respected and pious man, who worked in association with the famous Bubenburg family in the castle at Spiez, who, in their turn, were highly regarded and extolled for their honesty, should have merely invented this account.

Kyburger also places the beginning of the culture of the Oberland knights and shepherds in the first centuries A. D. The noble Ptolemaios, a wise man versed in all the sciences of that day, is said to have withdrawn into the alpine valleys as a Christian. The church at Einigen, which is dedicated to the Archangel Michael, is said to originate from his family, which lived primarily in the Spiez castle on the lake of Thun.

If we follow the chronicle, the Oberland became one of the most important birthplaces for the Christian Middle Ages: the gentry of Strätlingen and Spiez were even related to the founders of the first kingdoms, which emerged during the upheavals resulting from the migration of peoples. The mightiest families, who lived in the alpine valleys belonged to their clan and even the King of the early medieval Burgundy (888–1032) is said to have descended from this line. At times this kingdom spread to the Mediterranean Provence and influenced the culture of Northern Italy – probably because of its key position at the most important mountain passes. It enjoyed a pronounced independence towards the ruling powers in Europe and for this reason it was attractive to those people who valued freedom and sought for independent development.

One of the most beautiful legends that we possess from this time, and which found its way from the pages of the chronicler's book to the people, is the story of the dream of the Burgundian King Rudolf II.: Stricken by an evil scourge, he once saw how, in a vision, he stood before heavenly judges for his deeds and was to justify himself. The angels Gabriel and Raphael were good advocates to him, but the devil was also there and

_____

In the course of thousands of years, the Aare has forced a way through the rocks.

Page 16/17: Evening mood at the Spiez castle on the lake of Thun.

repeatedly found reasons against him. As the Good in his life was weighed up against the Evil and his love for the church at Einigen, as well as his promise to care for it more in future, was considered, Saint Michael let the scale tip in his favour. The King recovered thereafter and did everything to turn his alpine kingdom into a focal point of Christianity.

The same Rudolf II. saw the celestial city with its twelve portals in his dream; each portal was guarded by an angel. Due to this vision, and apparently equally inspired by the twelve jewels in the crown of his wife, the King had the twelve churches built around the lake of Thun, which are still standing today and which are described as «Burgundian». They are in the following places: Frutigen, Aeschi, Leissigen, Wimmis, Uttigen, Thierachern, Scherzligen, Thun, Hilterfingen, Sigriswil, Amsoldingen and Spiez.

The Burgundian King's attempt to transform his Oberland kingdom into a replica of the celestial fort by means of these shrines, is one of the most beautiful and moving of all the tales of the Middle Ages – even if it should lack all proof. Nevertheless, today's research into the 10th century accepts that an astonishing number of churches were built around the lake of Thun: as regards to the wife of the pious ruler, who was the famous Bertha. Today, when people get along in a friendly, peaceful and merry way, one still uses the saying: «It's like the times when Bertha lived here».

The daughter of Rudolf and Bertha was St. Adelheid, wife of the Emperor Otto I.; she lived until 999. Many blessings are said to have been given out by the whole family in this cheerless age; the «end of the world due to the growth in sin» was expected with the close of the first thousand years.

From the Burgundian Kingdom to the Supremacy of Bern

The «Burgundian Era of the Oberland» about which critical historical research knows much less than the legend which transforms this era into a «Golden Age», came to an end in the 11th century. The various powerful families began a bitter fight for inheritance and predominance and the people, who are supposed to have seen a symbol for paradise here suffered unutterably under this discord.

Berchtold V. of Zähringen was then appointed from the German-Roman kingdom, to bring a degree of order amongst these belligerent and estranged barons – since chaos in the vicinity of important mountain crossings has endangered essential highways. In order to have a strong back-up for his advances into the Alps, Duke Berchtold founded the town of Bern in 1191. The poor historical sources and the imaginative legend both report of manifold bellicose devices by which he forced the mountain knights to recognize his sovereignty.

As in the legendary times of the Burgundian kings, who withdrew from invasions into the alpine valleys, the defiant barons fled from their picturesque homes on the lake to the almost inaccessible hinterland. The knight of Mettenberg, the leader of the Grindelwalder, is said to have fallen in a battle against the Zähringer. Berthold V., however, is said to haunt the Oberland until this day, because he committed bloody attrocities in his attempt to reunite the Oberland valleys around the lakes of Thun and Brienz. Hartmut Radel deals with this in his guidebook: There are some people who claim to have seen him in splendid armour. The large buttons of his uniform shine so brightly, although it is pitch black, that they can dazzle and almost blind a man.

The history of Bern is full of occasionally contradictory details; for example how the town of Bern, founded in 1191 by the Zähringer, step by step consolidated its power in the Oberland and destroyed the family seats of the nobility in battle, or if these were already impoverished, merely bought them out. «Bern is the crown of Burgundy» sang the Bernese people. The «Handveste» which Emperor Frederic II. of Hohenstaufen gave to the citizens of Bern as early as 1218, contains the gift of very significant civil rights and liberties – this is explained by the simple fact that the German-Roman kingdom urgently required Bern and the roads into the Oberland for its security.

The people and particularly the Romantic historians and poets, who became interested in the tradition of the Alps in the 18th or 19th century, saw Duke Berchtold as more than a hero of the moutain battles: he achieved as much through his politics of peace as by the sword. Through marriage ceremonies he reconciled enemy families, who had been wrestling for power almost since the «golden» times of the Kings on the lake of Thun. It is said that Ita von Unspunnen and Walter von Wädiswil found their way to one another through Berchtold V., after all sorts of adventures.

A feast, organized by the wise Duke, is said to have achieved more than all the declarations of war, and the shepherds from long feuding valleys met annually from that time on, intermarried and regarded themselves increasingly as a people. From this understanding of communal enjoyment, a new richness is said to have

The interior of the Schadau castle near Thun. It was built between 1846 and 1852.

The charming Jugendstil interior of the casino in Interlaken, which was built in the 19th century.

come into the valleys; firstly, the combined defense of the inhabitants was more effective against conquerors, and at the same time, facilitated a peaceful stay for the increasing number of travellers, especially the pious pilgrims.

The Splendour of the Knights and Minnesingers around the Lake of Thun

The various connections which linked the aristocracy of the Oberland valleys and their mountain tribes with the great wide world, turned the Oberland into a field for world trade in the Middle Ages. Just one example: Berchold III. of Eschenbach, the owner of the beautiful castle of Oberhofen on the lake of Thun, supported Rudolf I. of Habsburg in his bitter struggle against Ottokar of Bohemia and in 1278 fought at his side in the battle of Marchfeld, east of Vienna. In reward he was given the permission to build a permanent settlement between the lakes of Thun and Brienz. The small town of Unterseen was the result.

However, the Habsburgs and the Eschenbachs later became estranged and one member of this family, Walter, was involved in the murder of King Albrecht I. on May 1st, 1308, while he was crossing the Reuss. Unterseen came under the rule of the victorious Habsburgs until the end of the 14th century. They also dominated in Habkern, Goldswil, Wilderswil, Lütschental and Grindelwald – in areas which had previously belonged to the Eschenbachs. In the Romantic period scholars believed that Wolfram von Eschenbach, one of the greatest poets of the Middle Ages, had also originated from this family line and this idea contributed to making the Bernese Alps and lakes into a destination for travellers at the start of the 19th century. This view of Wolfram's heritage, which is only based on a few controversial pieces of evidence, found little mercy with later academics – nevertheless the old belief in the Oberland as a home of medieval poetry does have some justification: The poet Hermann Hutmacher told me how he as a child in the Oberland had heard how the adventures of the knights in all the world «and above all love» were once extolled on all the feasts in the Oberland castles, particularly in Spiez, as late as 1955.

The Stretling chronicle from the 15th century tells of the chivalrous Heinrich von Stretlingen, how he

The elegant staircase in the «Victoria Jungfrau» Hotel in Interlaken.

«wanted to gain the friendship of the people everywhere in the surrounding area». He invited many people to his territory near the castle of Spiez and the church of Einigen, «noble and unnoble alike». There was singing, jumping, shooting, bowling, skittles, stone throwing, eating and drinking and sins of the sort which are committed at such festive times.

Heinrich von Stretlingen is well known as a significant Minnesinger, who lived in the 14th century and some of whose most beautiful sonnets are still known. His attempts to bring «noble and unnoble» together in communal feasts, proved to be a beautiful medieval dream of fraternity which ended in disappointment. According to the above – mentioned chronicle, discontentment developed from the inititialy joyous gatherings of various people. The rulers of the various Oberland territories are said to have soon forbidden their subjects to take part in such multifacetted feasts.

Another significant Minnesinger of this world of knights was Johann von Ringgenberg, the landvogt of Brienz (1293–1351). As a man of important connections – he accompanied Emperor Heinrich VII. and Ludwig of Bavaria on their journeys to Rome – he also possessed the right to live in the up-and-coming town of Bern.

Invincible Highlanders

Extant documents show the medieval Oberland families of Stretling (Strättligen), Bubenberg, Weißenburg, Scharnachtal, Eschenbach, Oberhofen, Unspunnen, Erlach all at the centre of world trade, quite regardless of where they had originally migrated from: They served kings and emperors as warriors, advisors and diplomats; they took part in crusades and pilgrimages to the Orient or fought with Tartars and Turks around the fortresses of Eastern Europe.

The adventurous folk of the surrounding area, strong and skilful through shepherdry and hunting followed them into faraway lands and there are countless legends which tell how they often received astonishing civil rights and liberties there from grateful rulers. For instance, corresponding tales amongst the

Page 22/23: Mighty and threatening the Eiger rises above the Kleine Scheidegg railway station (2061 m).

The railway at Brienz Rothorn. On the single track stretch of the railway above the lake of Brienz.

Haslital people are very wide-spread: They are supposed to have helped the German-Roman Emperor to rescue the city of Rome from an attack of the Saracens.

The legend of the village of Iseltwald on the lake of Brienz is delightful. The village is said to have rendered the whole of the Bernese Oberland great service when the German emperor was attacked by powerful enemies and sent a message to our highlanders, who had often aided him in battle. However, after a short consultation, the latter only let him have the «three giants of Iseltwald» with the remark, that each of these was of more use than a whole campaign of useless folk. And so the strong Oberland people defeated the hostile army and in return requested the grateful rulers to allow them to incorporate an imperial eagle in their banner, should their community ever become so strong that they could one day take the field with three hundred warriors. It is understandable that the medieval rulers did everything to uphold good relations with those people who lived in the vicinity of essential passes. Only those who possessed loyal allies on these

alpine crossings could easily go from the North to the South.

From the 15th to the 18th century these war-accustomed highlanders became mercenaries in European armies, especially as the population and the poverty of the areas increased. There was hardly any sort of disagreement at this time, in which warriors from the confederate communities, particularly from the alpine region, did not take part. It was often feared that certain valleys would bleed to death. The warriors from the mountains, the *Lütschentaler*, who undertook to guard the pope, for instance, were regarded as very reliable, physically strong and agile-minded. And so it was that, for the most part, they acted as watchmen, where «loyalty and determination» were no less necessary than in the tendering of cattle.

Mercenaries, who returned home, brought news from all over the world, and occasionally great knowledge to the otherwise remote valleys. Travelers were astonished to find men with whom they could converse in their own language in the lonely parts of the Alps! These mercenaries who had come back also helped to spread the reputation everywhere in the neighbouring countries, that there were enough people in their remote valley community who were

The mountain railways have been serving tourism since the start of the century.

familiar with the latest developments in the science of war. It is the people's belief that this was an important reason why Switzerland was seldom troubled by conquerors and, all in all, had enjoyed a certain peace since the time of the Murten war. Even Emperor Napoleon I., whose territory included the whole of Switzerland (1798–1815) granted them significant freedom – on the condition that they made enough of their famous soldiers available for his campaigns.

Those in Search of Happiness and Treasure

Shepherds on the lonely Alps, crystal seekers, treasure hunters, herbalists, root hunters and chamois hunters have all contributed to the imaginative legends of the Oberland. They preserved the legends of the old knights about the riches of the royal courts as far as the Orient and passed them on in a more elaborate form. The highlanders occasionally drew on these legends for their leisure; as a form of comfort as they battled to earn their living, which, all too often, was threatened by danger. For instance, as they waited for the end of harsh weather under overhanging cliffs, in caves or isolated mountain huts, they devoted themselves to the world of thoughts between dream and reality.

They watched the strange forms on the rockface and recalled the stories of the crystal rooms of the elfish «Earth and Mountain people», which were said to be deep under the earth. At times they even began to leaf through the yellowed books by natural scientists of times goneby, which had found their way into the remotest valleys and had been preserved there with great care. It was especially at times of economic crises, for instance in the 19th century when the manufacture of highly poisonous matches in the Frutigtal made many people ill, that an ancient dream surfaces; instead of wasting one's energy in endless toil and still living on the breadline, it should be somehow possible to find the entrance to the treasure cave – and thus escape poverty in one go.

Here the tales of the ancient migrations of the peoples and of wars, which during the treasures of Attila or of the Burgundian kings were buried deep in the ground, mingled with tales about bronze, gold, silver and jewels which «grew» in the ground. Tradesmen passing through with odd books, which were occasionally traced back to Capucin (monks) and gypsy magicians, found good customers in the highlanders. An old teacher from Adelboden told me in great detail how he saw a half dozen of these in the *Obere Simmental*, Diemtig valley, Engstligen valley and Kienvalley. As late as 1930 a peddlar told a folklorist from Thun how, in the crisis period at that time, he was able to sell a good fifty copies of such books on his trips «from Grindelwald to Meiringen» and «what's more only in the course of one warm season».

The content of these instructions for treasure hunting, still printed by a number of publishing houses today, has been charmingly summarized by the collector of legends, Hans Michel, in his book «Rund um den Schwarzmönch» («Around the Schwarzmönch»): «Only he who has never thought, spoken, or written untruth, never abused friendship in the slightest way, never turned a beggar down, never had unchaste dreams, never drunk one too many or said unkind things about others, can find gold. Hand on your heart before you dare such a thing, for neither the underground nor fire or water, air nor storm spirits let themselves be made a fool of.»

Digging for hidden treasures in the earth was not just pursued by adventurous souls or the financially desperate; before the influence of the French revolution of 1789, the government of old Bern, is said to have occasionally supported this sort of research. If we have been correctly informed, however, these attempts at mining in the valleys of Frutig or Hasli always cost more than they brought in.

One treasure hunter, a mysterious «Venetian», is said to have laughed aloud in Adelboden, when one miner told him of the expensive life: «Many a poor community», he assured the miner, «has more of riches on its land, than the whole of the city of Rome is worth.»

And so the old stories of the wonderful treasures in the often barren ground of the Oberland prove to be the presentiment of a great truth: In terms of health and happiness of the individual, it can give us gifts, which cannot be measured by all the money in the world.

Goethe at the Holy Waters

Folklore assures us that the Bödeli, the land between the lakes of Thun and Brienz, was already inhabited long before the Middle Ages. Scouts are supposed to have advanced into the mountain valleys from here and to have knelt before the magnificent miracles of creation. «Nothing but fountains!» is all they are said to have uttered, when they were asked for their impressions. This is allegedly how the name of the Lauterbrunnenvalley («Nothing but fountains valley») came about; in this valley the old villages of Zweilütschinen, Isenfluh, Wengen, Mürren, Gimmelwald tell of a rich history of inhabitants.

In the year 1779 Johann Wolfgang Goethe undertook his famous journey from the town of Unterseen to Lauterbrunnen, which at that time lasted a good three hours. He too admired the Staubbach stream crashing down from the height of the cliffs, no less than the first legendary immigrants of a thousand or even more years ago. Upon seeing this natural miracle, he is known to have declared «It is a most sublime subject» and the impression obviously awakened a number of religious associations in him.

The stream gushes from the mountains; if the weather is good, it seems as if it is falling directly from the blue sky down into the depths. We can quite comfortably draw nearer to the place where the waters reach the earth and enjoy the rare view as the sunlight transforms the fine splashes and the mist which forms in the warmth of the sun, into a haze of diamonds.

If it is hot in the Alps, one can see the steam rise and drift up to where the mighty waters crash down. If we devote some time to this observation we can see how a virtually unique impression arises from this play of the elements. It is as if we were watching a mysterious eternal movement, a cycle without beginning or end! It is as if the stream which gushes out from the heights, dissolves more and more under the influence of the air and the blazing heat of the sun, transforming itself into glimmering steam. This steam can drift weightlessly up to the heavens again, condensing again above the lofty cliffs, to be forfeited to gravity once again and to sink down towards the earth.

The stream inspired Goethe to his famous «Gesang der Geister über den Wassern» («Song of the Spirits over the Waters»). The waters cascading down over the rockface and the mist as it swirled upwards appeared to him to be a powerful allegory of human immortality. The soul comes down from above, descends into earthly matter, and then rises to the heavens again – this is performed in eternal rotation.

It has been presumed that Hegel in the same way gained one of his most important natural impressions in the Oberland – he was tutor to the von Steiger family

The seven steam locomotives on the Rothorn railway date from the 19th century.

Page 28/29: A winter evening in Zweisimmen, the regional centre of the Simmen valley.

in Bern from 1793 to 1796. While the great philosopher generally thought more practically and soberly than the alpine travellers of the enraptured Romanesque period, it is likely that he shared Hölderlin's enthusiasm. We know that the latter wrote the following to his «dear brother Hegel» in 1794: «I would like to have your Alps and lakes around me occasionally. Mighty nature ennobles and strengthens us irresistably.»

Goethe, Hegel and Hölderlin showed us a facet of the enthusiasm for the valleys of the Oberland, which induced poets and thinkers to travel to the alpine region around the lakes of Thun and Brienz. In the crisis years of the 18th to the 20th century especially, they traveled to see the most sublime views of the alpine mountains and found a timeless atmosphere here which gave them new strength.

In his play «Das Zentrum der Spekulation» («The Centre of Speculation»), written in 1840, K. Rosenkranz, who is known to be very influenced by Hegel, puts out a call to the philosopher: «When the mountain torrents roar into the valley, the yodel of the wayfarer rings out like a lark ... and the snow-crowned summits of the ancient mountains beckon with silent majesty under the stars. Oh then I truly feel that philosophy is only a language of symbols. Oh God, all speculation is merely a feeble imitation of your revelation».

Dreams about the Castle at Unspunnen

The legends of the mountain valleys as the sanctuary for people during times of crisis, in the era of early Christianity, the Burgundian kingdom and in the times of gruesome plagues, doubtlessly lived on into modern times. As the old order fell in ruins again during the French Revolution and the campaigns of Emperor Napoleon I., many people fled from the chaos-ridden cities into remote mountain huts.

The Confederation, in its previous form, was shattered by the invasion of the troops of the French Revolution in 1798. The city of Bern had put up a certain measure of resistance and was at first separated from «its» Oberland by the new rulers, precisely because they could gain many of their best warriors, some of the most feared mercenaries, from here: Because of this an independent canton arose around the lakes of Thun and Brienz for a short period.

However, many considered how this atmosphere of radical change, from which much of the discouragement and desperation arose, could be overcome. The individual sought his roots, firm foundations for a new beginning; no one quite knew what would come of it all. Nevertheless, it is important to note that the dream

of a miracle which would come from the Alps soon won many adherents – and not just in Switzerland!

People believed in the healing power of the alpine countryside on their souls and were convinced that the people from the Oberland offered an example for everyone; for they had shown in their long history that, by means of inventive genius and helping one another, they could survive even right next to the perennial ice, and even develop a liberal, independent life-style. At that time people thought of the pious legends surrounding the early years of Christianity on the Oberland lakes, of the «happy» Burgundian kingdom of the kind Queen Bertha, which had been transfigured by legends: Naturally, they also thought of Duke Berchtold of Zähringen. And so, due to a vivid dream of a rich history, the ruins of the old castle at Unspunnen, between Interlaken and picturesque Widerswil, became the scene of a feast of encounters and contemplation.

Urban scholars joined with alpine inhabitants to organise the much-cited «Days of Unspunnen», which first took place in 1806 and 1808; they were supposed to unite all those who still (or again) believed in youth and looked towards a creative future; there were poems and music. Strong men indulged in highland wrestling and the authentic mountain sport of stone throwing. Pretty girls danced in their colourful costumes.

In the Canton of Bern, to which the Oberland once again belonged, the astonishing feast had the effect to stimulate a reconciliation between the different classes: between the town and the country dwellers. It wasn't just admired in the whole of Switzerland; it had an incredible effect upon the neighbouring countries: the much-cited Madame de Staël, who exerted considerable influence on scholars in Germany, saw in it an appeal to the nations of Europe to reform their social life in a new way.

Today it is hard to imagine the degree of enthusiasm which the Alps exuded at that time and which drew alert people from all over the West in search of the spirit of true freedom. According to the Prussian Court Counsellor, Carl Gottlieb Samuel Heun, one can find one's most wonderful youthful dreams actually exist here. Under the pseudonym of Heinrich Clausen this best selling author wrote his sentimental (yet popular) Oberland novel, «Mimili» (1816).

The romantic-medieval castle at Oberhofen was once the home of a line of Burgundian aristocrats.

Page 32/33: The main town of the Bernese Oberland is Interlaken. In the background, the Jungfrau (4158 m).

A Dane, Jens Baggesen, composed his work «Parthenais» (1803) during his climb to the Jungfrau: Admittedly, he relied upon native legends, but he nevertheless believed, that he had all but discovered the countryside which corresponded to the European spirit. He even claimed that the Greek Gods could be encountered in the unspoilt countryside, almost as vividly as in the days of Homer.

A Destination for Poets and Philosophers

The enthusiasm for the countryside and the whole life-style of the Bernese Oberland now seized the Romantic poets – they lived in the hospitable, pictur-esque vicarages and sat together with the locals in the lounges. Their enthusiasm is reflected in their poetry or in the diaries of their journeys and appears to confirm the teachings of the old natural scientists and doctors. They confirm the latters' idea that even the air in the alpine regions can exert an enrapturing effect on the person who is receptive to it.

In the Oberland the English Romantic, Lord Byron, evidently forgot many of the gloomy, melancholy thoughts which tortured him in his lifetime. He even esteemed the dancing of the merry people of Brienz more highly than the corresponding arts in his English home: «The English cannot waltz, never could and never will be able to». He found the singing of the girls in Oberhasli almost perfect: «Their way of singing is wild and strange, but at the same time full of grace».

Some researchers have pointed out that even «Faust» reveals Goethe's impressions of his journey through Switzerland. Indeed, Goethe called Byron's comparable, magical-mystical poem «Manfred» (1817) «a description of the alpine countryside»: «The stage is in the Alps and in the other world». Immediately after the work had appeared one critic saw a clear correspondence with extant legends surrounding the ruined castles of the Bernese Oberland. It was soon presumed that Byron had almost definitely taken either Unspunnen near Interlaken or the Wimmis castle at the gateway to the Simmenvalley as the setting for his poem.

These and similar works found many fans, and soon whole throngs of people from the educated classes visited the country which at times was regarded as the actual home of poetry. The sight of the majestic Jungfrau, the wild streams crashing down, the reflec-tion of the stars in the pure water of the alpine lakes are said to have «washed away» the shadows of civilisa-tion.

In 1826 a poet of the class of Mary Shelley, who also belonged to the coterie of poets around Lord Byron who believed that truth could only be found in nature, published the utopian novel «The Last Man», which anticipated many of the subsequent English and American utopian dreams: In this novel, which is set in the 21st century, the continued existence of a morally degenerate humanity is endangered by a terrible and apparently quite unstoppable disease. Then Prince Adrian succeeds in withdrawing into the Alps with the vestiges of the English people; the absolutely curative air stops the seeds of decline. This way humanity is rescued and can now hope to experience a felicitous new beginning.

In as far as they could afford it, all classes now followed the mountain visionaries and poets. With every social crisis the rapidly growing number of Oberland guest houses filled with people from every country, in search of peace of mind. Many of the first pioneers of the rapidly expanding hotel trade even tried to give their new hotels something of the appear-ance of the old alpine huts and occasionally even of the legendary castles. Most of their guests were grateful; like Byron they still felt at the gateway to the «other world», near to the kingdom of happy dreams.

The Climatic Health Resort for all Europe

The wonderful air in the Oberland, which is said to redeem people from all suffering, was not solely disc-overed by healers and natural scientists of the last two centuries.

Existing documents prove that its miraculous powers had already been recognized at the time of the «noble and unnoble»; indeed they often traveled great distances to come to the Oberland lakes and to settle in the surrounding area. The Stretling chronicle, written towards the end of the Middle Ages, verifies this about the area around the castle at Spiez and the old church of Einigen: «… and the land and soil around Stret-lingen …, which also possessed a good, healthy air, better than one could find near or far. And for this reason it (this part of the earth!) was called the 'Golden Air' …»

A teacher called Alfred Bärtschi from Adelboden, who was very well-versed in legends, told me the wise words of a shepherd from the Haslital: «The old stories about the clever Venetians and the travelling doctors, who told the Oberland people that their land was full of riches, of gold and jewels, is perhaps only an alle-gory. Even the air that they breathe is a richness in

A wide panoramic view over the Frutigland. At the front, the village of Frutigen.

34

The wonderful crystal clear water of the «Blausee» in the nature park in Kandergrund.

itself, which explains why their land was continuously traversed by pilgrims, who sought and found health through arduous journeys».

The legend of the «Golden Air» finds a counterpart in the experience which a man suffering from tuberculosis told my uncle, Anatol von Steiger, in the 30s: Desperate and, as he had been told, incurably ill, he decided to stay a few weeks in an alpine hut near Gstaad. Suddenly on one beautiful morning it seemed to him as if the sunshine had transformed itself into «rain of gold and jewels». When he visited the doctor the next week, the latter spoke of a miracle, for a pronounced and completely unexpected improvement had taken place – the man is said to have recovered completely, to have married, had children and was admired almost everywhere for his fresh appearance.

Tales like this and the corresponding proof of them, the reliability of which has been vouched for by a number of eminent doctors, transformed, at least in certain decades, large parts of the Oberland into a single health resort. Almost every region which was famous at the beginning of the 19th century for its picturesque appearance and the world of legends which surrounded it, is now regarded as a place where one can breathe miraculously freely and allay all weakness and suffering.

For example, if the mountain torrent in the valley of Lauterbrunnen was first regarded as an ideal place for philosophers and poets to contemplate the secret of creation, it now became a rendezvous for those fatigued by civilisation. In 1897 the Russian doctor B. Tschlenoff assured his compatriots that all the factors of the natural environment combined to heal their contemporaries, who had been weakened by civilisation: «The woods in the surrounding area fill the air with fortifying balmy vapours. The waterfall itself and the lake beneath it give the air the necessary humidity and in the hot summer days convey the uplifting freshness and coolness».

Let us take one further example of the climatic medicine of the previous century; real renewal was said to take place on the Axalp, which stands by the Faulhorn: the doctor Körber sent those convalescing after long and grave illnesses here, to live in wooden alpine huts. He also sent children here whose physical development was behind that of their age group.

One could compile such details one hundred times over from the old travel journals and to one's great astonishment, one would establish that our great-grandparents expected no less than that which those in the distant past expected from the healing effects of the fantastic «Stone of Being».

Guests in the Wooden Huts and Castle Hotels

Everything had combined to generate the travel spectacle as the unquestionable highpoint of the 19th century. Moreover, it seems almost all the world – from North America to Russian-Asiatic Siberia – participated. The well-developed Bernese Oberland had become a popular holiday destination.

The philosophers, poets and those dreaming of freedom were the first to go; they were followed along the ever wider, better paved roads by all. In order to prove their rapport with tradition, even the most widely-read authors had to write books which would induce their readers to merrily undertake trips to the Alps. In his tales the French writer, Alexandre Dumas, mixed his own adventures with legends which he had partly heard from others or which had been partly elaborated by him. He did this in such a way that the

At an altitude of 1578 metres in the foothills of the Dolderhorn lies the Oeschinen lake.

two can hardly be untangled today. With the tales of his travels about mountainous Switzerland, its glaciers and sunrises, the American writer, Mark Twain, created one of the most amusing books of the century.

The very successful English writer, Arthur Conan Doyle, is said to have pondered long and hard over which one of the picturesque places in the Oberland he should place his master detective Sherlock Holmes in for his last decisive encounter. Ultimately, he decided upon the Reichenbach falls. There are still numerous ladies and gentlemen from the Anglo-Saxon world who annually visit our mountains merely to follow the traces of their hero. Many people even believe that he actually existed in real life.

If the Oberland lakes were regarded as a country of peace towards the end of the Middle Ages, which pilgrims could cross on their way to holy places quite

Page 38/39: Alpen horn blowers on the Almenalp above Kandersteg. In the background, the Blümlisalp.

undisturbed, the same region now became famous as an «island of happiness». The stately homes on the lake of Thun, which were still modelled on the originally medieval castles at Spiez, Oberhofen or Schadau near Thun, or the new palace hotels became meeting places. Before the First World War, the latter, with their external flourishes and interior comfort were much admired; later they were dismissed as «bourgeois kitsch» … (Today in Interlaken and in other places where they have not fallen victim to subsequent rebuilding, they are regarded as moving monuments of the «good old times»!

In a Europe of feuding powers influential people from the most disparate backgrounds met, often under poetically sounding code names. They encountered each other politely beneath the heavy chandeliers of fashionable hotel corridors, drank expensive champagne together or undertook daring tours in the mountains which could often degenerate into playful shows of courage between Englishmen and Russians, Germans and French. Together they visited the climatic health resorts and the spas of the various «magic mountains» which were supposed to improve their health and got to know their mutual strengths and weaknesses. They undertook coach journeys, lit by romantic torch light, to the picturesque beauty spots or watched as the lights were lit on the mountains on feast days or how the waterfalls were illuminated by colourful rockets. Love affairs between people from different countries, who normally regarded each other with great mistrust, developed and for many years mountain crystals or wooden bears from Brienz, given as keepsakes, were preserved in decorated caskets. In other words: If, after all the world wars and revolutions, the last century today seems to be the era of a certain peace and flourishing of culture, it is largely explained by the social, human and often personal reasons inherent in the migration of peoples within the Bernese Oberland.

Artists, politicians and businessmen met here in their relaxed leisure time, without a record of their conversations being held. They got to know and understand each other here and the Oberland made a rare contribution to developing a broad circle of Western culture: the representatives of various communities met one another while pursuing the same pleasures, admiring the same natural beauty spots, resting by the same stoves in the alpine cabins.

Timeless Atmospheres

«If you manage to quickly climb to the point where the base of the rainbow touches the earth, you will find a golden pot full of jewels, all as colourful and gleaming as the rainbow itself. With this gift from heaven, as one used to say to children, you can make your fortune.» So the tale was told to me on the Alp Seefeld, high above Interlaken in the heart of the Oberland.

There is one other related story which was known, so an old man from Adelboden told me, in Saanenland as well as in the valleys of the Frutig and the Hasli. Could it be ancient and rooted in the fairy tales of all the migrations of the peoples? Did it emerge from the phantasies of those artists who stayed in the Alps? Was it a product of those poets, who in the 19th century sought romantic reminders of the vanished kingdom of fairies and elves – Byron, Shelley or Scott?

«If you succeed in walking underneath (!) a rainbow when it stands like a bridge across the valley, then you will see the countryside behind it like an earthly paradise. Everything is just the same as it is here, but the colours of everything are more radiant, just like the beautiful rainbow itself and the flowers in the meadow, from which the cows gain their particularly good milk.» He who has experienced such a miracle is said to be prepared to do everything to regain the same impression from the alpine countryside. As if enchanted, he is compelled in future to seek out a place in the mountains, from where one can view the wonder of the colours in a new way.

Of course, this is «only» legend or superstition, but no doubt borne from genuine and intense experience, which explains why shepherds, chamois hunters and those in search of crystals or herbs often became «addicted» to their often dangerous mountain paths and strayed into melancholia, far from their homes. Modern day walkers experience something similar, if they walk along the ancient tracks in the Oberland and return there every year from that point on: There is probably no better symbol than our legend for the enchanting, colourful variety of creation in the Oberland – it gives every individual with alert senses exactly that atmosphere which he has been seeking since his childhood and which fills him with deep joy when he is in the reality of the Alps.

And so the symbol of this legend is the very best interpretation for the fact why people from all directions visit the Oberland so regularly. Whether they are mountain climbers, skiers, health seekers or happy walkers – they find those impressions and atmospheres today, which undoubtedly belong to the most beautiful natural wonders in the world.

Well organised and secure paths allow easy and difficult mountain tours around the Oeschinen lake.

Traveller's Guide for the Bernese Oberland

Six Routes by Car and Eleven Walks
Compiled by Gertrude Reinisch

The most simple way to approach the Oberland is by motorway from Bern to Thun. A motorway-vignette is required to use the motorways in Switzerland; for a fee of 30 Francs the vignette is valid for one year and includes the use of all inland tunnels up to a length of 19 kilometres. However, the traveller who wishes to see more of the country and its people and who has sufficient time at his disposal, will decide in favour of taking the passes and country roads. The romantic, well-tended villages, weathered wooden houses, enchanting lakes and the immediacy of the glittering glaciers put every traveller into a holiday mood after only a few kilometres.

He who prefers to arrive feeling well-rested will choose to travel by train. Almost all of the main towns and ski resorts can be reached by rail even in winter. One of the most charming scenic alpine railways in Switzerland is the Montreux – Bernese Oberland line (Lake Geneva – Gstaad – Zweisimmen – Spiez – Interlaken). It employs the adhesion principle (friction) to overcome the steep gradient; it needs neither a cog system nor a cable system in contrast to the railway from Lucerne to Interlaken (via the Brünig pass and Meiringen) – which is still partially dependent on a cog system.

The nearest international airport is Zürich-Kloten. There is also an airport in Bern. Apart from those in Interlaken and Gstaad-Saanen, there are some other miniairports which cater for small aeroplanes; however some of these are closed in winter. «Air Glacier» offers sightseeing flights, helicopter skiing and, in summer, guided tours of the glaciers.

Public transport in the Bernese Oberland means: In addition to convenience, short waits and great comfort, public transport offers the chance to get to destinations, which are inaccessible by car or are closed to public traffic. But all the other places can also be easily reached by bus or train. We recommend travelling by ship on the lakes of Brienz and Thun.

The three-or-four pass journey by mail bus along the passes of Susten, Grimsel, Furka, and Brünig is particularly impressive and restful. The approach road from Reichenbach to the Griesalp is closed to private cars and it is the steepest route which any mail bus uses. Similarly, it is only the mail buses which are allowed to drive over the Große Scheidegg; Wengen and Murren are also closed to cars and can only be reached by the rack- or cablerailway. A time-saving device is to use the motorrail train to travel through the Lötschberg tunnel. Those who wish to travel further south, can continue their journey by rail through the Simplon tunnel.

Six Routes by Car

If we look at the distance, which is to be covered on the individual excursions, we will see that the kilometres are few. However, if one wants to see everything, one day for one route will hardly be enough – three days or more will probably be needed. Whoever doesn't have so much time, should pick out a few «gems»!

Route 1: Around the Lake of Thun
Interlaken – Thun – Spiez – Interlaken (51 km).

The area around the lake of Thun is often described as the «Riviera of the Bernese Oberland». The climate here is extremely mild. Fourteen holiday resorts lie on the sun-lit slopes around the lake. The countryside around the lake of Thun belongs to some of the most delightful and varied for walking in Switzerland. The footpath around the lake of Thun offers walking fans the opportunity to investigate the area in stages by Shank's pony. From a trip on one of the twelve boats views encompassing the banks of the lake and the 4000 metres height of the Bernese alps can be seen. The lakeside resorts can be easily reached by train or bus. Fans of history and local history can find many fortresses and castles around the lake. Romantics can ex-

---

Above Saanen, one has a glorious view on to the summits of the Vorder- and the Hinter-Eggli.

Page 44/45: At the Simmen falls at the end of the Obersimmen valley lies the Oberried valley.

Hay harvest near Kandersteg. On the left, the summit of the Bire (2502 m).

perience picture-book sunsets within the «blue-green pearl» of the Bernese Oberland. For those interested in water sports there are many possibilities: bathing, sailing, surfing, water-skiing, diving and canoeing are just some suggestions. The sailing school at the lake of Thun is the oldest in Switzerland and has three branches (Hilterfingen, Spiez and Interlaken-Neuhaus). Other sailing schools can be found in Gunten and Thun; waterskiing schools in Faulensee and Gunten; boats can be hired in Gunten, Hilterfingen, Interlaken, Leissingen, Merlingen, Spiez and Thun; diving schools can be found in Gunten and Interlaken; windsurfing schools can be found in Faulensee, Gunten, Interlaken, Spiez, Thun and Därlingen.

The tour begins in *Interlaken*, which lies at a height of 570 metres between the lakes of Brienz and Thun at the foot of the Bernese Alps: it is the ideal starting point for trips into the Bernese Oberland.

Der *Höhenweg* is for Interlaken what the Champs-Elysées is for Paris or what the Kurfürstendamm is for Berlin. A 700 metres long boulevard with hotels,

souvenir shops, exclusive boutiques, numerous parks and squares and splendid flower beds. It leads from the east station to the west station, passing the Höhenmatte, with the famous view of the Jungfrau.

The beginnings of tourism in Interlaken go back to the 15th century! In 1836 the first steamer traveled across the lake of Thun. From 1872 to 1874 the Bödeli railway was built between the two lakes – one of the very rare two-story railways in Europe. In 1893 the lake of Thun railway was opened.

In approximately 1133 a monastery was founded here. Within a short space of time the monks were the largest landowners in the Bernese Oberland. In 1257 a convent was affiliated to it. In 1528, when Bern changed to the faith of the Reformation, the monastery was abandoned; today it is the home of the regional administration. The monastery courtyard of the former Augustian rectory, with its gothic cloister, the castle church from the 12th century, the chancel from the 14th century, the horseshoe-shaped castle gardens from 1757, the old townscape of Unterseen, historical farmhouses in Matten are all worthwhile destinations of a tour of the town.

In *Unspunnen* one can find the derelict castle ruins and the meadow, where the famous shepherd feasts

took place in 1805 and 1808 – the last one was in 1981. Unspunnen is still the centre of Swiss traditions and the place where the famous Tell open air performances (based on Friedrich Schiller's play) about the foundation of the Confederation, are held.

Since the 19th century, Interlaken has been one of the most frequently visited tourist resorts. Well-marked footpaths and zoos can bring a little variation to your holiday. In winter there are well-prepared footpaths for tranquil excursions into the countryside and numerous cross-country ski runs are marked for skiers. Natural and artificial ice rinks are available.

The *Heimwehfluh* houses the fantastic lay-out of the model railway, which was modelled on the railways at Gotthardberg and Lötschberg. A 600 metres long slide and a 30 metres viewing tower offer an unforgettable experience not just for children. The evening tours to the *Harder Kulm* are attractive for their traditional entertainment. The tourist-museum in *Unterseen* should also be visited.

Soon after this little town with its pretty townscape and the typical urban wooden houses we come to *Neuhaus-Weissenau* (nature reserve). Weissenau was once the castle built in water for the barons of Weissenburg.

Pleasant hikes can be undertaken by the Oeschinen lake from the chair lift station «Lager».

Further along the northern bank we reach the *Beatus caves*, a place of pilgrimage from the 15th century. The Beatus grotto is a prehistoric settlement in drip stone caves. The path leads through fairy-tale like caves, past raging underground waterfalls and splendid stalactites.

High above the lake stands the farming village of *Sigriswil*. The church tower from 933, the gothic font, the community vaults from 1564 and the museum of local history are worth seeing. The Sigriswil ridge is a good place for climbing. In autumn the famous *Kästeilet* (cheese sharing) takes place in Justistal.

Along the lake the road leads down to *Gunten*. This little village lies at the foot of a wild romantic ravine with a waterfall and at the delta of the Gunten stream. Old houses, built in the typical Oberland style and the storehouse in the centre of the village are the most distinctive features of this popular centre for windsurfing.

The journey goes on to *Oberhofen*. The emblems of this village are the castle with its valuable collections, the splendid castle park, the vine slopes and the *Heidenhaus* (house from pre-historical times). The grounds of the park, which border right on to the lake, lie in one of the most charming gardens in Switzerland, which includes botanical rarities. The keep originates from the 12th century, the palace is medieval. Between the years 1849 to 1852 a drastic reorganisation took place. The interiors are magnificent and are taken partly from Bernese town houses. The castle at Oberhofen was once the residence of the barons of Oberhofen and Scharnachtal, in the 17th and 18th century of the Bernese *Landvogtei*, and then later a private residence. The decoration offers an overview of all the styles since the Middle Ages. This stately home is open from the middle of May to the middle of October. From June to August concerts take place in the castle.

Almost without a transitional journey we arrive at *Hilterfingen-Hünibach*. The noteworthy pre-Reformation church probably goes back to the 7th or 8th century. The current building was erected in 1727. Performances of folklore take place in the wonderful grounds at the castle in Hünegg from June to August. The park grounds also include a Jugendstil museum.

Following the course of the River Aare from the lake of Thun we reach the town of *Thun*. This charming old town is called the «gateway to the Bernese Oberland». The medieval centre, the castle with the museum, old churches and buildings invite to undertake a journey into the past. The Wocher-Panorama, a unique circular painting (30 × 7 m), was painted in 1810 by Marquard Wocher. Along the main street with its high pavement, one reaches the *Rathausplatz* (town hall square). The town hall was built in 1589, converted in 1686 and has an interesting archive. The castle, built in 1191, is an imposing keep with four round corner towers. The *Amtshaus* (administration building) was built before the castle in 1429. Old coats of arms and folk art are displayed in the historical museum and *Rittersaal* (knights hall). The art museum of the town is located in the *Thuner Hof*. Significant wall paintings can be found in the castle at Schadau. The castle was built from 1848 to 1852 and shows an original mixture of various style motifs; gothic themes dominate.

The picturesque Zähringertown possesses a Reformation town church, which was newly built in 1738. The front tower, dating from the year 1330, stands on the castle hill. The Scherzlingen church was built as early as the 8th century and was decorated with particularly beautiful wall paintings from the 13th and 16th century. This church is a prime example of Romanesque architecture; the frescos are, however, of Gothic origin.

Alongside many other events, the cellar theatre and the barrel organ festival provide entertainment in Thun. At the beginning of the autumn holidays the *Schützenfest* (traditional shooting festival) takes place. Particularly the *Gesslerschiessen* (cross bow shooting) should not be missed. The first festival of this kind was as early as 1551.

We continue our tour around the lake along the southern bank. We soon reach the idyllic village of *Einigen*. The emblem of this village is its thousand years old church, the mother church of all Romanesque churches in the region of the lake. The font is of particular interest due to the Bubenberg shield from the year 1446. The wide Kander delta, overgrown with reed and the «Gwattlischenmoos» provide a home for many different varieties of birds.

In the next bay of the lake lies *Spiez*, nestling between hills and vine slopes. It is dominated by the castle of the Strättliger, Bubenberg and Erlach families. The foundations of the keep probably originate from the 10th century, the upper part, the palace and north wing from the 13th century. The extension of the keep took place in 1598. The castle contains a museum with living- and reception-rooms from the 13th to the 18th century.

The former parish church Saint Laurentius, together with the vicarage and the medieval grounds of the fort, form a picturesque silhouette of unique beauty. The church is an early-Romanesque new building, erected around the year 1000. The Carolingian tower may have been built as early as 700. The baroque extension took place in 1670, its restoration in 1949/50. The flat-roofed basilica with its square pillars, three naves, three part choir and upper chancel as well as wall paintings from 1200 and 1500 is unique. The well-known and well-loved Spiez wine (Riesling-Sylvaner and Blauburgunder) thrives on the Spiezberg. A vine pickers path leads across the vine slopes. Concerts at the castle, open air performances and festivals of folklore are annual cultural high points in Spiez.

Faulensee, once a wine growing village, has developed into a fishing village and is the meeting point for experts and fans of culinary delicacies from the lake. A romantic, shady beach path leads to Spiez. The modern church and the excavations of the Columban chapel should not be overlooked.

A little distance away from the high terrace lies *Aeschi*. The glorious panorama of the mountains in the Kander valley and onto the lake is the reward for

Goats on an alpine pasture close to Betelberg-Leitli near Lenk in the Obersimmen valley.

From the Jungfraujoch, the view stretches across the Aletsch glacier as far as Wallis.

---

this excursion. In the «Aeschistube» in the old *Gemeindehaus* (community hall) next to the old church, agricultural and domestic utensils as well as kermis carving and peasant painting can be admired. The church originates from the 13th century and has beautiful frescos as well as choir seating which is richly decorated with carvings and marquetry.

Guided tours of the mountains and visits to the alpine cheese-making factories are offered. Aeschi is a good starting point for a visit to the romantic «Suld-Pinte» in the Suld valley. A water-wheel and special paths where one can learn about plants and the woods should not be missed in Suld. Ski lifts, a cross country ski run, a natural ice rink and a ski school encourage one to take one's winter holiday there.

Somewhat remote from the route lies *Mülenen* in the Kander valley. The name of the wild stream, Kander, is derived from the Celtic word Kandara, which means «the white goddess». One only needs to observe how the Kander thrashes down upon the rock face up in the valley, to understand why the Celts gave

it this name. The longest permanent cable railway in Europe (3,5 km and with a gradient of 68%) travels from Mülenen to the Niesen (2362 m), the most beautiful vantage point on the lake of Thun. Even Johannes Brahms once enthusiastically climbed the Niesen, the pyramid of the Bernese Oberland.

We return to the Lake of Thun by way of *Krattigen*, which is a popular spot in spring because of its unique cherry blossom. We travel on to *Leissigen*. This quiet fishing village consists of pretty Oberland houses and still has an historical set of buildings, consisting of a church, vicarage and barn, which make up the centre of the village. Above the village there is the memorial for the painter Ferdinand Hodler.

The last village in the tour around the lake of Thun is *Därligen*, at the foot of the Därlig ridge. A generous peripheral road keeps through traffic distant, and so it is quite quiet in the little idyllic place.

Route 2: Around the Lake of Brienz
Interlaken – Iseltwald – Giessbach – Ballenberg – Brienz – Oberried – Interlaken (49 km)

By dint its wild, romantic setting the lake of Brienz is of unique beauty. While the left bank is edged by steep

The Jungfraujoch (3454 m). On the right, the high alpine research building on the Sphinx cliffs.

mountain slopes, the other side is dominated by hills, crowned by green alpine meadows and rocky ridges. The lake of Brienz is one of the cleanest stretches of water in Switzerland. It is also said to be very rich in fish. Trade and pleasure ships travel across the lake as well as a nostalgic paddle-steamer. Boats can be hired in Boenigen, Brienz, Iseltwald and Giessbach.

From Interlaken we travel along the southern bank to the spa of *Bönigen* and then further to the fishing village of *Iseltwald*, which stands on a peninsula and invites one to take a picturesque stroll along the lake side to *Giessbach*. Giessbach is well-known for its fish specialities. The high point of every trip around the lake of Brienz by paddle-steamer «Lötschberg» is a visit to the Giessbach falls. The water masses cascade in fourteen falls to a depth of 400 metres into the lake – an extraordinary natural spectacle.

A short trip to the *Axalp* (1600 m) is worthwhile. In this village, which is especially suitable for families, one can enjoy traditional alpine meals and performances of folklore. Axalp is also the departure point for big game excursions. In winter torch-lit descents are an attraction to skiers.

We travel on by means of the narrow country road to *Kienholz* and *Hofstetten*. Right next to the carving

village stands the famous *Ballenberg Open Air Museum*. A very faithful copy of the most beautiful old farmhouses in the whole of Switzerland were reconstructed here and convey an exact idea of the rural lifestyle. In the 50 hectares of grounds the houses of the individual regions were united in groups and surrounded with gardens and fields. The museum is open from April to October.

The buildings in the village of *Brienzwiler* date in part from the 16th century and through their formal unity they offer an insurpassable picture of a village.

Brienz, the main resort on the lake, can be reached in a matter of minutes by means of the expressway. The name Brienz first appeared in 1146, under the description «Briens» – which roughly means «hill». Brienz has become known throughout the world for its wood carving and violin making schools. An unusual attrac-

Page 52/53: The emblems of the Bernese Oberland in the evening light – Eiger, Mönch and Jungfrau.

Barn on an alpine meadow of the Alpscheidegg in the vicinity of Grindelwald.

tion is a journey on the ninety year old steam railway – the only one in Switzerland still running to a definite timetable – to the Brienz Rothorn (2350 m) with its glorious view. A 2 kilometres long promenade along the lake side, the village museum and the old part of the village are a journey into the past. In the wildlife park stags and chamois can be observed. Trips to view medicinal plants, alpine festivals with hunting and shooting in an alpine cabin are offered.

We travel back to Interlaken via the spas of *Eblingen, Oberried, Niederried, Ringgenberg* and *Goldswil* on the northwest bank of the lake. In *Ringgenberg* the early baroque church was built from 1676, using the keep of the medieval fort as a church tower.

Route 3: The Two Pass Journey
Giswil – Brünigpass – Meiringen – Handegg – Grimselpass (63 km)

The little village of *Giswil* between the lakes of Sarn and Lunger lies in the northeast extremities of the Bernese Oberland. The *Brünigpass* (1008 m) can be reached around a few bends and via the village of Lungern at the southern tip of the lake of the same name. The altitude is just right for getting used to the highland. Soon after the pass is the turn off left in the direction of *Meiringen* (595 m), and the entrance into the *Haslital* (Hasli valley), *Hasli* comes from *Hasler*, the harsh, medieval population of the valley, who travelled along the old mule tracks across the passes and undertook, controlled and occasionally also «ruffled» the transportation of wares. Numerous sayings and legends are woven around the freedom-loving and tradition-conscious *Haslitaler*.

Although the area is only small, the Hasli valley offers everything which one expects of an alpine region: mountains, glaciers, water, ravines, alpine meadows and passes. Meiringen lies 2100 metres below the Grimsel pass, and the Hasli valley is an ideal channel for the famous-infamous *Föhn*. In the course of the past centuries the village had burnt down to its foundations. And so it is not surprising that the *Föhn* today still dominates many of the everyday rules of behaviour.

The first thing that one sees is the beautiful old church. It was built in 1684 upon the old outside walls

of a late romanesque bell tower. These date from the 13th century. Alpine meadows, saturated with flowers and wonderfully aromatic mountain woods line the village with its old wooden houses. The famous Reichenbachfall offers a wonderful spectacle. It unifies the waterfalls of the Rosenlaui. A cable car travels up to the waterfall. A memorial shield to Sherlock Holmes hangs at the cable car station. The spiritual father of the legendary detective, Sir Arthur Conan Doyle, was so impressed by the wildness of the falls that he eternalized them in his books. In the Hasli valley Sherlock Holmes not only withstood adventures, but reported that he was most taken with the delicious meringues, the recipe for which is still guarded like a state secret by the bakeries.

It is not much further to *Rosenlaui* with its spectacular glacial gorge, where the Weissenbach tempestuously springs forth. The views of the wild crags of the Engelhörner make the heart of every climber beat a little faster.

Any way of hiking is possible in the Hasli valley. There is a weekly programme for daily excursions with a guide. The mountain climbing school in Meiringen also offers climbing and glacier tours. Those who prefer it a little less wild can walk along the well-

In the angular village lanes of Wengen above the Lauterbrunnen valley.

marked footpaths. The three hundred kilometres of footpaths are a unique opportunity, even in Switzerland.

Meiringen possesses a pleasant Hasli museum, interesting church excavations, a natural history collection and a crystal museum. There are also public festivals: In July the *Brünigschwinget* and the *Nidlete* on the Mägisalp, in August the village festival in Käserstatt and in September the *Käseteilet* on the Mägisalp.

The parts of the village which lie on the «first storey» of the Hasli valley are at a height of 1100 metres. The villages Hohfluh, Wasserwendi, Goldern and Reuti or Käserstatt can easily be reached by cable-railway or via the road to Brünig. The *Sennen* (dairy men) work on the Mägisalp in summer. There one can watch how the «Hasliberg mountain cheese» is made. For *Zniini* (inbetween refreshment) there is mountain cheese, milk and bread. It is also worthwhile visiting the hand weaving works in Meiringen and Oberhasli.

Just a few kilometres outside Meiringen the next surprise awaits us – the Aare ravine. From *Innert-*

kirchen, well-known passes lead into the neighbouring cantons, Uri (Sustenpass) and Wallis (Grimselpass). This link between north and south was important even in the Middle Ages. Wonderful crystals are hidden in the rock walls of Oberhasli. The most beautiful quartz, crystal and minerals can be admired in *Guttannen* on the road to Grimsel. The exhibition is open from June to September. The road zigzags its way up the mountain to the Hotel and Restaurant Handegg, which stands at an altitude of 1408 metres and which has become a meeting-point for climbers. A cable-railway leads from there to the high alpine Gelmer lake, and the path to the Gelmer cabins acquaints the walker better with the wild highland landscape.

The momentous panorama over the mountain tops, covered in névé, becomes ever more impressive. After every bend new views across the glacial lakes and reservoirs open up: the lakes like dark green eyes between the gleaming black, mighty cliffs and above these are white masses of ice, towering up, which have been rolling towards the valley for thousands of years. Before the road was built (in 1894) it was an adventure to cross this pass and the road builders' achievement is clear; the road enables us to experience the natural spectacle so comfortably, *Grimselhospiz* on the fjord-like reservoir (1909 m) offers a favourable spot for staying overnight, just a few kilometres beneath the pass (2165 m). The pass can only be used in the summer months from June to September and in autumn until the end of October. The maximum gradient is 9%.

Route 4: Excursion into the Region around the Jungfrau

Interlaken – Zweilütschinen – Grindelwald (23 km). Zweilütschinen – Lauterbrunnen – Wengen – Stechelberg – Mürren (43 km)

The first place after Interlaken on this journey into the Jungfrau region is *Wilderswil* with its Gsteig church from the 8/9th century. Elements from the Romanesque, Gothic and baroque styles dominate the form of the church today. While the church was being renovated, wall paintings from the early Middle Ages were discovered. The licencing rights of the hotel standing at *Bärenplatz* go back to 1714. Opposite stands the enchanting *Bärenhaus* from the 16th century. The old mill with the water wheel is to be converted into a museum. An experienced collector of minerals will assume control of it, adding his collection of crystals, which belongs to the largest in Switzerland.

The cog railway to Schynige Platte was opened as early as 1893. The view from here onto the Bernese mountain giants is fascinating. It is definitely worth

taking a stroll through the gardens of alpine plants (it is one of the oldest in Switzerland). Guided tours and botanical excursions are offered and at the end one can partake of a typical «Oberland refreshment» in the mountain restaurant. Those who would like to get to know a little more of the area, should not stay here too long and should travel along the Lütschine to *Zweilütschinen* (654 m). There we turn off left towards *Grindelwald* (1050 m). Courageous conquerors of the peaks have carried the name of this neat mountain town, at the foot of the famous north face of the Eiger, to all corners of the world. Where else can one observe the acrobatic achievements of mountain climbers, as they climb the icy steep face, which still counts as one of the most difficult in the world, from one's hotel terrace, binoculars in hand and over a glass of beer? Once the jagged icy peaks and the crevasses of the glacier reached right down to the edge of the village. Later the two natural spectacles of the glacial ravine and the ice grotto were made accessible to tourists.

More than three hundred kilometres of prepared and marked footpaths and hiking paths lead across sumptuous meadows, through spicy aromatic fir woods and past effervescent mountain streams at numerous vantage points.

In spite of the large number of tourists, Grindelwald has remained small and cosy. Shopping streets with small shops offer countless Swiss specialities, such as the legendary Swiss Hotel cheese.

Public festivals take place in July on the Männlichen (Alpigelen alpine festival and the spring mountain festival of Männlichen), on the Grosse Scheidegg (mountain festival) and on the Bussalp *(Chilbi)* and in August on the Aellfluh *(Chilbi)* and on the Männlichen *(Chilbi)*. It is traditional for individuals to meet each other for a friendly «measuring of strength» at these festivals, according to exactly prescribed rules. This is called the *Schwinget* (wrestling gala).

A superlative on this route is the journey on to the *Jungfraujoch.* The highest placed railway station in Europe (see walks, Tour 6, p. 68). In the second valley of the Lütschine lies *Lauterbrunnen*, which is fairly well-known for its lace making. Seventy-two waterfalls go down over the rock face – thereby giving the village its name *lauter Brunnen* (nothing but fountains). This valley with its impressive waterfalls, is also a natural and wildlife reserve and, as such, is an ideal centre for moderate mountain hikes or highland tours, which are organised by approved mountain guides. It is quite

---

From the Hotel «Lauterhorn» in Wengen, the view stretches across the Lauterbrunnen valley.

possible that the famous Staubbachfall is admired and photographed more often than the Niagara falls. It cascades over the Mürrenfluh and is visible for a long way.

Inside the mountain the Trümmelbach falls rage five hundred metres down into the valley with deafening noise. Seven glacial waterfalls drain the glacier faces of the Eiger, Mönch and Jungfrau. Every year they transport more than twenty tons of debris. By means of a tunnel lift, a covered walkway and viewing platforms one can watch this impressive, well-lit water spectacle.

Lauterbrunnen is the ideal point of departure for trips to the villages *Wengen* and Mürren, which are both closed to cars. The last village in the valley is *Stechelberg* (867 m). The Untersteinberg/Breitlauenen nature reserve invites one to take a peaceful walk in a quiet area, far away from the tourist villages. Those who wish to view the Schmadribach falls at close range, should not forget to take their umbrella.

To end the day it is worth making a quick trip by cable railway on to the Schilthorn and to *Mürren*. Mürren is an ideal centre for walking. Since the James Bond film «On Her Majesty's Secret Service» (1969) the Schilthorn is also known as Piz Gloria and is a popular destination for excursions. From the modern revolving restaurant one can see as far as Jura, the Black Forest, Lake Geneva and Lake Constance. Mont Blanc, too, can hardly be missed.

Route 5: Through the Lötschberg
Spiez – Kiental – Frutigen – Engstligental – Kandersteg – loading station – Lötschenpass – Goppenstein (87 km)

The *Frutigland*, with its many branching valleys is one of the most beautiful parts of the Bernese Oberland. The most unspoilt of these valleys is probably the secluded *Suld valley* with its sleepy villages and nature and plant reserve. This is the home for twenty different types of orchids, ten sorts of gentian, fields full of Turk's cap lily, over three hundred chamois antelopes and numerous protected species of bird which are threatened by extinction. The Pochtenfall is a worthwile destination for a hike, which can be reached quickly.

From Spiez, the important village of *Reichenbach* (707 m) is eight kilometres away. Amongst the most important sights is the village centre with its houses from the 15th century. The covered wooden bridges across the Kander (Schützenbrücke and Reudlenbrücke) the crystal cellar situated in the market place, the Jakobea Stucki craft weaving studio in the resplendent Stuckihaus, the vantage point at Geissboden, Faltschen and the Jüsihaus in Scharnachtal with its

impressive gamekeeper lounge. Reichenbach is also the home of the bow makers and box painters.

From Reichenbach we take a left turn to the *Kiental*. Griesschlucht, Tschingel lake, Hexenkessel, splendid waterfalls and Griesalp (which can only be reached by post bus from Kiental!) are just some of the most important scenic landmarks. We travel back to Reichenbach and from there to Frutigen (803 m). The late Gothic church is noteworthy here. It stands on foundations from the 10th century and was rebuilt in 1726. The organ dates from 1809. Houses typical of the Frutigland, which were built in the 16th to 18th century, and the ruins of the Tellenburg castle dominate the appearance of the village.

We travel on to the right towards the *Engstligen valley*. Seven kilometres along the road are Cholorenschlucht and Pochtenkessel, both good places for a shady walk. The last larger village in the valley is the spa town of *Adelboden* (1353 m). The neat wooden houses of this mountain village are situated on something of a sun terrace. The church was built in 1433. The *Jodlerchilbi* on the Tschentenalp in June and the barrel organ festival in August offer a source of ethnic entertainment. Alongside its high attraction factor, as one says in the business, Adelboden also offers various drinks which are said to encourage good health. At the end of the street which leads through the valley, a cable car travels to the Engstligenalp, past the Engstligen falls and also offers an impressive view of the glaciers of the fascinating mountains.

We travel back to Frutigen and up towards the Kander valley. The village of Kandergrund is but a short distance away. A little further, the first attraction of the valley awaits us – the blue lake by *Mitholz*. This lake with its dark blue, crystal clear water lies in the middle of a wonderful natural park. Boat trips, romantic strolls, the breeding of alpine trout, documented by a photographic show and the best culinary trout specialities count amongst the greatest enticements. In the region of the Riegel lake there is a game park and St. Bernard dogs are bred.

The village of *Kandersteg* (1176 m) lies high up in the Kander valley. The various sights take some time to see: the village church from 1510 with its old paintings on the ceiling vault and carving on the chancel, the plate bearing a coat of arms, the Ruedi house, richly decorated with sayings and ornaments, from 1753, the facade of the Hotel Ritter, the old saw mill water wheel and the Klus Kander falls. Impressive hiking paths

The church at Frutigen. This village was completely reconstructed after a huge fire in 1827.

allow one to glimpse into the mountains of the valley. In summer a wood festival and a shepherds festival take place on the Gemmi as well as the Blausee-festival. High above Kandersteg, a cable car ride away, lies the Oeschinen lake, which is situated at the foot of the imposing group of mountains formed by the Blümlisalp, Fründen and the Doldenhorn group. A little fast water canoeing down the Kander into the lake of Thun may attract the adventurous.

The loading station for the «Rolling Road» through the Lötschberg tunnel is also in Kandersteg. Cars are transported (at reasonable rates) at short intervals (15 to 30 minutes) to Goppenstein (Wallis).

Route 6: Through the Simmen Valley
Spiez – Wimmis – Zweisimmen – Lenk – Gstaad – Lauenen – Les Diablerets (142 km)

The town of Spiez on the lake of Thun is once again the point of departure for this walk. The Simmen valley takes its name from the Simmen falls (the «seven fountains») and stretches from the narrow part of the valley in Wimmis up to the Iffigen lake and the Simmen falls. Nestling between Stockhorn and Niessenkette, it is the mildest and longest valley in the Bernese Oberland. The houses from the 17th and 18th century in Diemtigel, Boltigen and Därstetten provide examples of perfect wooden architecture. The Simmen valley also became famous for its race of speckled cattle.

The first village in the Simmen valley is *Wimmis*, centred around its castle. The medieval grounds of the castle were extended in the 17th century. The keep and the walks along the battlements belong to the oldest parts of the village. The church originates from the 10th century. This early Romanesque building is famous for its three-naved basilica, with its square pillars and three apsides. In the middle of the 15th century both rows of pillars were removed. The late Gothic wall-paintings originate from the 15th century. We follow the street through the unspoilt farming land with its charming villages and old farms, the emblem of this countryside, past sumptuous meadows and pastures.

Erlenbach (700 m) is a holiday spot for hanggliders. The Stockhorn is the ideal starting point for this sport. In a matter of minutes the cable car glides up to the summit. A hundred kilometres of prepared hiking paths allow extensive mountain tours; canoe and dinghy boat trips satisfy those with an adventurous spirit. Anglers can find their booty in the river Simme and the Stockhorn lakes. Due to its famous, medieval frescos the church in Erlenbach counts as one of the most beautiful rural churches in Switzerland. The Romanesque foundations of the current church go back to the 10th and 11th century, the spire of the choir originates from the 13th century. Due to sparse light and the massive dimensions of the building, the interior still gives a very medieval impression. The late Gothic wall-paintings belong to the best examples of Gothic *Gesamtdekoration* in Switzerland.

The centre of this stolid Simmen valley village consists of magnificent farmhouses. The Vépy and Hofer houses of the main village street are particularly well preserved.

The Knuti house in Moos near *Därstetten* was erected in 1756. It is a well-proportioned and richly-decorated building and is regarded as one of the most beautiful farmhouses in Europe.

The next village is called *Weissenburg* and is famous for its mineral springs. The village of *Boltigen* follows shortly on the connecting road to the Jaun pass.

In *Zweisimmen*, at the foot of the Waadtland alps, we take the left hand fork towards the *Obersimmen valley*. We reach *Sankt Stephan* via Blankenburg and Riedhäusern. The mountain municipality has organised one hundred and fifty kilometres of walking paths.

The next high point of this trip is the moulins in *Lenk*. Two hundred kilometres of marked hiking paths lead through wildly romantic countryside punctuated by dangerous ravines. The spa town of Lenk lies in the green mountain countryside at the foot of the snow-covered Wildstrubel. A trip to the Simmen falls near *Oberried* at the end of the valley and to *Iffigenalp* should not be missed.

In order to travel to *Saanenland*, we go back to Zweisimmen, turn left and travel to *Saanenmöser* and *Saanen*.

Music fans from all over the world travel to the annual Yehudi-Menuhin-Festival. For those who like to go hiking, the western region of the Bernese Oberland offers a wide array of routes. Peaceful rambles or demanding tours of the mountains are possible. Mountain trains bring the numerous tourists to a height of three thousand metres.

The chicest place in the Bernese Oberland is *Gstaad*. The rich and famous meet in this holiday resort on the German-French border. The breadth of the Saanenland stands in great contrast to the narrow

The members of a folk dancing group wait for their performance on the Hasliberg.

Page 62/63: A cheese maker. In the Ballenberg open air museum, old craft techniques are demonstrated.

valleys and gorges in the rest of the Bernese Oberland. Here the countryside opens up and forms a harmonious transitional passage to the hilly Waadtland alps. In a side valley, seven kilometres away from Gstaad, lies the small spa village of *Lauenen* (1241 m) with the Geltenschuss waterfall. Through the romantic Gelten valley (natural reserve), one can stroll along to the picturesque Lauenen lake, an oasis of peace for the city dweller, who is plagued by stress. The winter holiday maker can choose between good downhill slopes and two cross-country ski runs.

The Best Walks in the Bernese Oberland

Walk 1: Saanenland
Lenk (1068 m) – Trüttlisbergpass (2083 m) – Lauenen (1241 m). Five hours, gentle mountain hike.

This pleasant walk across the passes, by means of well-marked mountain paths, mainly traverses alpine pastures from the upper Simmen valley to the Lauenen valley. The path is without problems and easy to find.

The best thing to do is to travel by train from Spiez to Lenk. From there we take a northwesterly direction across Flöschweid, Sulzig and Siten to the *Oberen Lochberg* and climb up to the *Trüttlisberg pass*. The view on to the Wildhorn and Wildstrubel is fabulous. After climbing for a thousand metres, however, a longish rest is necessary.

We descend via the *Vorderen Trüttlisberg* and *Rütschli* to *Lauenen*. The post bus takes weary mountain climbers back to Spiez. The usual walking equipment is needed for this trip: sturdy mountain shoes, comfortable clothing, a pullover and waterproof clothing.

Walk 2: Simmen Valley (Two Day Tour)
First day: Zweisimmen (941 m) – Seeberg lake (1831 m) – Schwenden (1163 m). Seven hours, easy mountain hike.
Second day: Schwenden – Otternpass (2278 m) – Achseten (1067 m). Seven hours, easy mountain walk.

First day: Departing from Spiez we travel by train to the lower Simmen valley to *Zweisimmen*. From there we walk into the lonely *Diemtig valley*. The well-marked path, with its excellent position, leads to the natural reserve. The picturesque mountain countryside with its steep, rocky summits and deep blue lakes, bedded in soft, rich alpine pastures with their bright mix of flowers is enough to make every walker enthu-

siastic. However, because there are no suitable places for breaking the journey on this tour, one should have a little experience of mountain climbing and be steady footed. One should also be fit enough. The usual walking clothes are adequate. A warm pullover, waterproof clothing and food and drink should not be forgotten. Water can be refilled in the clean mountain streams. Mineral drink powder and lemonade tablets should also be taken along: they replace the salt and minerals which have been sweated out and prevent cramp in the calf muscles. It is important that strength is conserved for the next day.

From Zweisimmen we take the steep uphill path to *Stierenberg* and *Seeber lake* (the highest point!), which lies at a height of 1831 metres. Via *Meniggrund* we follow the stream gently downhill to *Zwischenfluh*, the day's destination. Once we have arrived, we can go to the accommodation reserved for the night. Should the weather be bad or if one has blisters, one can travel by bus back to Oey-Diemtigen and from there by train to Spiez.

Second day: We walk into the Diemtig valley on the footpath next to the road as far as *Schwenden*. At the Grimmi alp rest home we take the left-hand fork and follow the stream to *Otternpass*.

This walk traverses the most beautiful alpine region in the upper Diemtig valley – via the Kilei alps and across the Niesenkette between the wild Gsür and the Manniflüh, which commands such tremendous views. After a rewarding rest at the highest point of the day we walk slowly down to *Achseten*. From here it is possible to take the post bus from Adelboden to Frutigen and then the train to Spiez.

Walk 3: High above the Lake of Thun
Hilterfingen (560 m) – Heiligenschwendi – Teuffental – Schwarzenegg (916 m) – Honegg (1546 m) – Eriz – Horrenbach – Teuffental. 7 hours, gentle hike.

This mountain hike does not make any alpine demands on the walker; it merely requires a little stamina. On hot summer days this walk can also turn into something of a fight against thirst; for this reason it is better to select one of the enchanting early summer or autumn days.

Hilterfingen-Hünibach stands on the lake's right bank at a height of 560 metres and stretches to a height of 860 metres. This picturesque village extends over two and a half kilometres of park-like countryside at

The cheese yields of the pasture in one summer at the «Käseteilet» on the Hasliberg.

The Iffig falls in the natural reserve can be reached on foot from Lenk in one and a half hours.

---

the lake side. In the 16th century Hilterfingen was a wine growing village. Individual houses in the old centre of the village still indicate this. Now no grapes ripen on the meadow slopes, which are known for their mild climate. Distinguished country houses with exotic, rare trees command a splendid view.

The walk leads through woods and fields across the wild Zulg to Schwarzenegg. Then one reaches *Hüniboden* via Burech and Halten, «Bim Scheulus» (1009 m). From there one reaches the highest point of the tour, *Stalden*, at a height of 1162 metres. We go down a little to *Eselsteg* (745 m) via *Burghalten* and *Teuffental* and cross over the Zulg. Now the last uphill climb to *Schwarzenegg* (916 m) follows. About four hours is needed to get this far; that is if one does not stop to take in the overwhelming views over the lake of Thun and the Bernese alps or call in at one of the friendly inns on the way. Before beginning the way back, one option is to launch an attack on the summit of the *Honegg* (1546 m). To do this one walks for two hours along the marked path steeply uphill and finally

across the crest to the highest point. The steep climb downhill to *Eriz* is murder for the knees and it is almost a pleasure to see the compensation ascent towards *Horrenbach* after crossing the Zulg. From there it is not much further to *Teuffental*, where we rejoin the earlier path and walk back to *Hilterfingen*. Towards evening it is also worth making a little detour between Teuffental and Heiligenschwendi to the vantage point at *Blumen*, to observe the sunset. The last stage of this walk is already known and can also be finished when darkness is falling. For the sake of safety a pocket torch can be taken along.

Walk 4: Frutigland/Alpiner Höhenweg Ueschinengrat
The station at Kandersteg/Stock – Winteregg – Gällenengrat – Gellihorn – Weissfluh (2472 m) – Schwarzgrätli – Schwarenbach. One-day mountain tour.

Experienced walkers can take the seven kilometres long path (at a height of 2200 m to 2400 m) from Stock to Schwarenbach. The starting point for the new path in the Gemmi region is the mountain cable car station at Kandersteg/Stock. After a short transitory passage the actual *Höhenweg* begins near *Winteregg*. After about

one hour we reach the Gällenen ridge, the first vantage point. From here a small detour can be undertaken to the summit of the *Gellihorn*. The path then leads on to the summit … from here one has a glorious view over the surrounding mountains. Especially in the first half of July, the sumptuous alpine meadows are a unique carpet of flowers. The path leads on to the *Weissfluh*, which (with its height of 2472 m) is the highest point of this highland hike (and offers a good view of the Wallis alps and Gemmiland). We continue across the *Schwarzgrätli* down to the *Schwarenbach Mountain Hotel*. The high path ends here. The well-built path is a new link between the cantons of Bern and Wallis. It can be walked from about the end of June to the middle of October when the weather is good. Good, sturdy shoes and waterproof clothing are recommended.

Walk 5: To the Blümlisalp
Kandersteg (1176 m) – Oeschinensee (1578 m) – Blümlisalp (2834 m). 4 to 5 hours, mountain tour.

This route leads into the magical world of the high mountains and is just right for dreamers and romantics. However, experience of mountain climbing is an absolute prerequisite. For those who don't have this

Hay harvesting on the Iffigenalp in a neighbouring valley of the Obersimmen valley.

experience, it is a good idea to follow a mountain guide. There is a local mountain climbing school.

Kandersteg lies at the foot of giant, fossilised and glaciated mountains. A chair lift saves one walking up to the *Oeschinen lake*. However those mountain climbers who are particularly athletic can easily overcome the four hundred metres ascent. At the lake we enter into the impressive mountains of this area. Dark faces of rock surround the small, deep blue Oeschinen lake. Gleaming white crags of glacier hang down threateningly deep; one can hardly imagine that there is a passable way through here. But at the end of the lake the path leads through a ravine to *Oberbärgli* at a height of almost a hundred metres, high over the lake to *Hochtürli* and to the *Blümisalp Hütte* on the edge of the Blümlisalp glacier. The hut stands far above the beginning of the glacier, which stretches down to 2300 metres. The sensible positioning of the path enables one to view the glacier from all sides.

Only those who wish to go further up than the hut need go into the glacier, as well as securing themselves with rope and climbing irons. The Weisse Frau (3652 m) is a worthwhile destination. But even those who walk back into the valley the next day and choose the high path through *Abeweid* above the Oeschinen lake, will probably never forget the sunrise and sunset in the gleaming glaciers of the Bernese Oberland.

Walk 6: Eye to Eye with the North Face of the Eiger
Interlaken (1570 m) – Grindelwald (1034 m) or Wengen (1275 m) – Kleine Scheidegg (2061 m) – Jungfraujoch-Station (3454 m) – Eiger glacier – Kleine Scheidegg – Walk along the high path to the Männlichen (2343 m) – Grindelwald. Gentle hike.

This gentle hike leads across the mountain crest between the Schwarzen Lütschine valley (Grindelwald) and the Weisse Lütschine valley (Lauterbrunnen). The paths are very well marked and well constructed. Neither a previous knowledge of the alps nor special equipment is required, for this hike can be comfortably completed in one and a half hours. It is actually more like a walk, albeit at the height of two thousand metres. Clothing for the hike should be chosen in accordance with this fact. Even in summer it can be quite cool, especially if one makes a detour to the 3454 metres high Jungfraujoch. Nevertheless, it is advisable to acclimatise oneself and get used to the height a few days in advance, so that one can bear the high altitude better, before being transported by cog railway into the ice labyrinth between the Mönch and the Jungfrau.

It makes little difference whether one sets off from Interlaken, Wengen or Grindelwald. The Bernese Oberland railway travels from each of these places up to the *Kleine Scheidegg*. There one encounters the crowds of tourists, observing the possible «death candidates» on the north face of the Eiger through binoculars. From here the Jungfrau railway travels to the Eiger Glacier station (2320 m). This stretch of the cog railway was opened as early as 1898. The station at the Eiger face was finished in 1903, the Eismeer station (3160 m) in 1905. It was only in 1912 that the fantastic work on the railway to the Jungfrau ridge was finished. In an almost superhuman achievement a tunnel (7,1 km length), serving a railway of 9,3 kilometres was blasted from the cliffs. Numerous «windows» in the tunnel, which were once used to dispose of building debris, allow the tourist alarming glimpses into the Eiger's black wall of ice and of the blinding glaciers above the level of snow. The cog railway can travel stretches which have a gradient of up to 25%. A lift brings one even higher than the highest cog railway station in Europe, the *Jungfraujoch* to the Sphinx terrace

(3573 m). Next to the Jungfraujoch Restaurant there is a tiny summer skiing resort with a short drag lift. Skiing equipment can be borrowed.

Passing the Grindelwaldblick Hotel, which is well-known from all the films of the north face of the Eiger, one follows the path along its horseshoe bend around the rocky ridge of the Lauberhorn. Climbing gently uphill, one walks along the east flank of the Tschuggen and follows the comfortable panoramic path to the mountain station of *Männlichen* (2222 m). Only half an hour is needed to reach the highest point on the Männlichen and one is again rewarded by a glorious panorama. Using the same path one climbs downhill to the 6,2 kilometres long cable railway between Männlichen and Grindelwald, which also has special compartments for those in a wheelchair.

The descent via the intermediary station of Holenstein (942 m) lasts about thirty minutes. Because the altitude changes so rapidly, one's ears may pop and one needs to swallow repeatedly, in order to hear again properly when one is down in the valley. Those who find this a little too comfortable can walk down into the valley on foot. It is still possible to change onto the cable railway in Holenstein. An asphalt street (built for those in a wheel-chair) and a natural track lead into the valley. The natural track is definitely preferable and one's feet will be thankful.

Walk 7: Across Grindelwald
Schynige Platte (2100 m) – Faulhorn (2681 m) – Bachalpsee (2265 m) – First (2200 m). 4 to 5 hours, mountain hike.

The cog railway has been travelling from *Wilderswil* onto the *Schynige Platte* since 1893. Even from the time mountain climbing was regarded as «madness» the viewing platforms over the whole of the Bernese Oberland have attracted tourists the whole year round. The railway brings its passengers through the wood across alpine meadows, thick with flowers, to the viewing platform.

Even cable car fans, who have only seen the Matterhorn from the Gornergrat and the Mont-Blanc from the Aiguille du Midi, are fascinated by the view: the closed wall of the giant Bernese mountains across the dark green valleys of Grindelwald and Lauterbrunnen

---

The old wooden house in the Bernese Oberland is decorated with flowers.

Page 70/71: Green alpine meadows and lonely mountain farm. On the right, the Bussalp (2020 m).

attracts all eyes. A stroll through the splendid garden of alpine plants, one of the oldest of its kind in Switzerland, forms the overture of the tour. The botanical knowledge that one gathers there can soon be deepened in the open fields, for soon we are walking through the typical flora of the primitive rocks; purple gentians, blue and yellow monk's hood as well as rolling fields of alpine roses from June to August. The fact that these plants adapt extremely well to the local conditions enables them to survive at the highest altitudes. The only threat to them is from people, as can be seen on this path by the decline in the various species.

Gradually the path leaves the busy Schynige Platte and traverses the southern flank of the *Laucherhorn* (2230 m) – a short trip to the ridge is rewarded by a great view over Interlaken and the lake of Brienz. Then the path leads on over the *Sägis valley* with its contained pond and over the crest of the *Sägissa* to the *Männdelen Guest House*. From here we can see up to our destination, the *Faulhorn*. The hour, that is usually necessary for this stretch, easily turns into a contemplative hour and a half, because from the summit ridge the «Group Portrait with Jungfrau» can be studied in all its detail. On the extreme left stands the Wetterhorn, then come Schreckhorn, Eiger, Mönch and Jungfrau. After walking for three hours the terrace at the Faulhorn Hotel offers you the chance to relax. This hotel on the summit has been defying the alpine wind and weather for 150 years.

The onward trip is downhill. Just after the delightful Bachalp lake the path forks. A sign indicates that the left hand fork leads to the chair lift station at First. This is an enticing offer for weary walkers who want to save themselves the walk down into the valley. Those who still have energy can take the right-hand path through alpine meadows and sparse woodland to *Grindelwald*. We travel back to Wilderswil by train.

Walk 8: In the Rosenlaui Region
Rosenlaui (1328 m) – Glacial ravine – Dossenhütte (2663 m) – descent into Urbachtal (838 m). 8 to 9 hours, demanding mountain tour.

The mountain tour is also organised as a guided hike starting at *Meiringen*. The silver gleaming summits of the prominent Wetterhorn group can be experienced from very close distance. Starting at the *Gletscherschlucht Rosenlaui* (glacial ravine) we climb up into an impressive rock landscape between Engelhörner (2782 m), Gstellihorn (2854 m) and Dossen (3138 m), finally reaching *Urbansattel* (2489 m). Passing the Biwak and crossing the narrow ridge between the Reichenbach and Urbach valleys we arrive at Dossen-

hütte after about four to five hours. Experience of mountain climbing is not necessary for the way down either. After two or three hours one is quite weary when one arrives in the Urbach valley.

Walk 9: To the Grimsel Pass
Grimselhospiz – Lauteraarhütte (2392 m). 4 to 5 hours, protected climbing path.

For this hike into the nature reserve one needs to be steady-footed, have a head for heights and mountain experience. At the same time this is one of the most beautiful and impressive climbs up to the huts in the Alps. From *Grimselhospiz* we follow the stairway steeply down on to the dam wall of the *Grimsel lake*. Following the dam wall we arrive at the granite plateaux on the other side of the lake. Wire cables and dents in the rock allow one to climb a little further. At the same time one can observe how serious mountain climbers climb about on the vertical rock face. Deep down below lies the lake, as we advance along narrow rocky paths. One can already hear the raging waterfall from far away; a small wooden footbridge leads past it.

In early summer some parts of the path are quite dangerous because of the remnants of old snow; climbing irons and an ice axe should be used. If necessary, one can improvise with a sharp stone. At the end of the lake we come to the so-called «El Dorado». In the vicinity of this six hundred foot high lump of rock, it is as though one has been transferred into the American climbing paradise of Yosemite. Adventurous hikers can try their first steps on warm granite at the foot of the granite plateaux.

We arrive at the *Lauteraarhütte* via the moraine on the north side of the Unteraar glacier. From this point one comes into the heart of the Bernese alps and can wander from hut to hut or climb the impressive summits. Those who have no ambitions in this direction, can simply walk back to Grimselhospiz the next day.

Walk 10: Through the Aareschlucht
1 hour, very easy.

The Aareschlucht (Aare ravine) is 1400 metres long and 200 metres deep. It constitutes an unforgettable

---

Mürren, high above the Lauterbrunnen valley. Eiger, Mönch and Jungfrau in the background.

Page 74/75: The Upper Grindelwald glacier, which stretches down into the valley.

The mighty summit of the Mönch (4099 m), photographed from the Schynige Platte (2101 m).

natural experience due to its grottos, niches and rocky vaults. It is open from April to October.

A rocky bar, a mighty wall of rock, called the Kirchet, stands between Meiringen, Willigen and Innertkirchen, a last vestige from the Ice Age. When the glacier reached much further into the valley, deep cuts developed under the ice. Debris and water still wear away the rocks inexorably. Over thousands of years the water of the young river Aare forced itself, gurgling and roaring, increasingly deeper into the rock, until the obstinate ravine, with its niches, grottos and basins had developed. Today one can walk quite safely by means of footbridges and tunnels through this unique natural spectacle.

Walk 11: To the Hochstollen

Meiringen (595 m) – Hasliberg – Planplatten (2245 m) – Balmeregghorn (2255 m) – Melchsee-Frutt (1900 m) – Hochstollen (2480 m) – Hohsträss – Käserstatt – Mägisalp – Bidmi – Mountain railway at Meiringen. Walking time varies, one-day trip, gentle hike.

This simple mountain tour can only be accomplished in one day by using the various lifts. They lead mostly through a charming alpine region with idyllic little mountain lakes and picturesque pastural cabins. The views of the glacial mountains in the surrounding area are very impressive. From *Meiringen* we quickly come to *Planplatten* via Reuti, Bidmi and Mägisalp. A well-marked path leads across meadows towards *Balmeregg*. Behide the *Rothorn* (2525 m) we climb a short stretch through the Firn valley and, in a few minutes, reach the summit (2255 m) of the *Balmeregghorn*. To reach this ridge about one hour is needed.

Not so very far below lie the deep blue mountain lakes of *Melchsee-Frutt*, Tannalp and Engstlenalp. The white-red-white track leads across the lake dam to Blauseeli. From this point it is all uphill. On the left the dark Fulenberg stands out. At the Spätbühel one can recognize a long corridor with a deep cleft, the Witries. Our path continues towards Tschugglen. A short, steep uphill path leads to *Abgachütz* (2222 m). Then we walk on towards *Hochstollen* and after a three hours

Near Grindelwald, one of the large winter sports centres in the Bernese Oberland.

climb, reach, rather wearily, the summit. The descent to *Hohsträss* (2119 m) is easy and doesn't even take an hour. One can take the lift again to Käserstatt (1840 m) or walk directly to Mägisalp.

The Best Areas for Winter Sports

The *Weisse Hochland* (between Zweisimmen and Châteaux-d'Oex) including the recommended resorts Gstaad, Zweisimmen, Saanenmöser, Schönried, Saanen, Rougemont, Château-d'Oex and Les Diablerets. 250 km of prepared slopes, 69 lifts, glacier skiing, position between 947 and 3000 m, 80 km cross-country ski runs, toboggan runs, ice rinks and glacier flights.

The *Diemtig valley* and the *Niedersimmen valley* including the resorts Boltigen, Oberwil, Weissenburg, Erlenbach and Wimmis. 30 km of prepared slopes, 15 lifts, position between 700 and 1868 m.

Adelboden and *Lenk*: 190 km of prepared slopes 44 lifts, position between 1068 and 2330 m, 40 km of cross-country ski runs, ice rinks, dog sleigh sleighing.

Kandersteg: Two small skiing areas between 1100 and 2000 m and 75 km of cross-country ski runs.

Jungfrau region: the skiing resorts around Grindelwald, Wengen and Mürren. 165 km of prepared slopes, 43 lifts, lies between 1050 and 2790 m, glacier skiing, 48 km of cross-country ski runs, tobogganing, ice rinks, helicopter skiing.

Meiringen-Hasliberg: At the foot of Susten and Grimsel pass. 50 km of prepared slopes, 13 lifts, lies between 595 and 2245 m, 35 km of cross-country ski runs, ice rinks, horse-drawn sleighs, toboggan run.

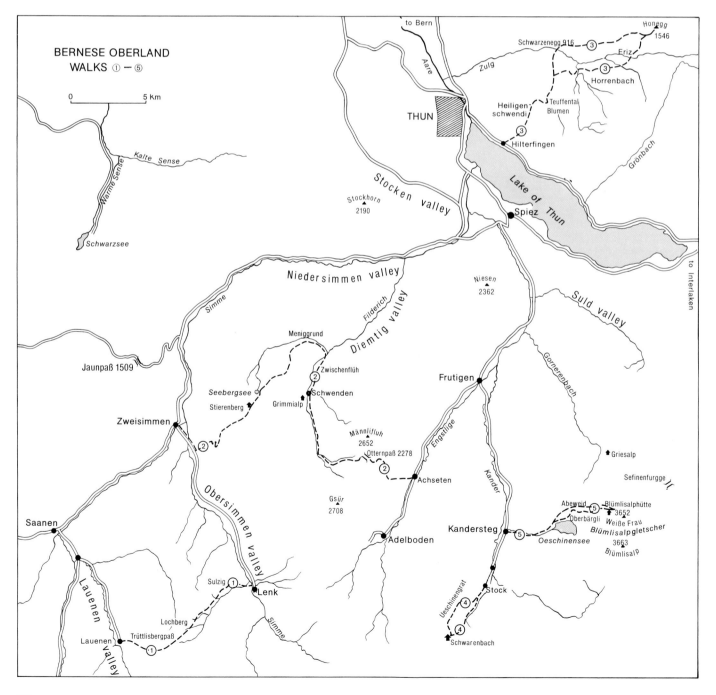

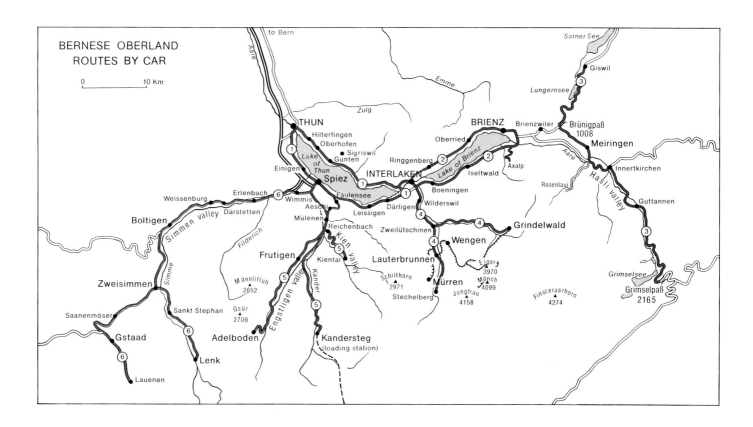

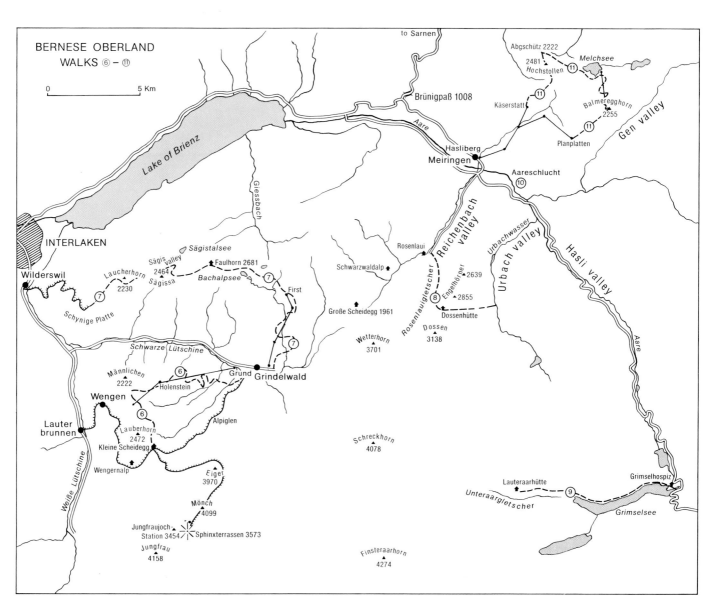

Illustration Editor: Axel Schenck
Translation: Rose Lord
Reader: Rüdiger Dingemann
Layout: Peter Schmid
Productioner: Angelika Kerscher

© 1989 by Verlag C.J. Bucher GmbH,
Munich and Lucerne.
All rights reserved.
Printed and bound in Germany
ISBN 3 7658 0615 3